Language and the State

Revitalization and Revival
in Israel and Eire

Edited by
Sue Wright

MULTILINGUAL MATTERS LTD
Clevedon • Philadelphia • Toronto • Adelaide • Johannesburg

Library of Congress Cataloging in Publication Data

Language and the State: Revitalization and Revival in Israel and Eire
Edited by Sue Wright
Also available as Vol. 2, No. 3 of the journal *Current Issues in Language and Society*.
Includes bibliographical references.
1. Language policy–Israel. 2. Language policy–Ireland. 3. Hebrew language–Revival.
4. Irish language–Revival. I. Wright, Sue.
P119.32.I75L36   1996
306.44'95694-dc21   96-39544

British Library Cataloguing in Publication Data

A CIP catalogue record for this book is available from the British Library.

ISBN 1-85359-385-0 (hbk)

Multilingual Matters Ltd

UK: Frankfurt Lodge, Clevedon Hall, Victoria Road, Clevedon BS21 7SJ.
USA: 1900 Frost Road, Suite 101, Bristol, PA 19007, USA.
Canada: OISE, 712 Gordon Baker Road, Toronto, Ontario, Canada M2H 3R7.
Australia: P.O. Box 6025, 95 Gilles Street, Adelaide, SA 5000, Australia.
South Africa: PO Box 1080, Northcliffe 2115, Johannesburg, South Africa.

Printed and bound in Great Britain by Short Run Press Ltd.

Contents

Language and the State: Israel and Ireland

Sue Wright
Institute for the Study of Language and Society, Aston University, Birmingham
B4 7ET, UK

A betting man in 1900 might have hesitated before wagering much on the probability that there would exist — by the mid-century — the independent nation state of Israel, with Hebrew as its language for public life, or the independent nation state of Éire, with Irish as an official language. Both projects would have seemed immensely unlikely in the context of the power of the British and Ottoman empires. It is against this background of the achievement of an ambitious political goal that the question of language revitalization in the two situations has to be studied.

The organising principles of nationalism are complex and much disputed.[1] There is profound disagreement over the relative weight of the various factors at work. However, it is perhaps defensible to claim, that belief in common ancestry, possession of common traditions and history (actual or invented), residence on a common territory, participation in a common belief system and communication through a common language have each played a significant role in the formation of nations, and that these elements interact with each other in different ways to produce the specificity of the various nationalisms. In the two cases, Ireland and Israel, that we considered in this series of CILS seminars, and which are recorded here in this issue of the journal, there appear to be certain superficial similarities in the inspiration for the national movements. For powerful majorities in both Ireland and Palestine, the wish to be with members of their own religious group and to be governed by a state organised according to the principles of their own religion were powerful motivating forces.

Language was not, at first, a defining characteristic in either case. In the Israeli context, the new Jewish settlers in Palestine were multilingual immigrants from four continents living side by side with the autochthonous population, mainly Arabic speaking. No single language was the obvious choice as lingua franca for the settlers, although Yiddish was the language of the culturally dominant group, and Hebrew had sometimes been used as a lingua franca between Jews from different linguistic backgrounds (Glinert, 1991). However, as soon as the movement had the goal of establishing a Jewish nation state in Palestine, a means of communication within the group became a prime requirement. A common language is an essential in any exercise in group formation: there must be a 'community of communication' where a polity aims to represent a nation, and claims legitimacy through that representation. Clearly the idea of 'Israel' would need a medium both to realise the dream and then to cement the reality. Professor Spolsky's paper recounts how Hebrew came to be that medium.

In Ireland, the shift to English from Irish was already firmly in place by the end of the nineteenth century (Hindley, 1990). Despite this, Irish was still a living language and, in theory, ready to be harnessed to the independence movement, both as a symbol and as the means of realising a distinct 'community of communication' separate from the British. In the event, Irish was to remain largely a symbol, and the majority of Irish chose English as the language for informal and formal group use in an independent Ireland, although all citizens were presented with the choice of Irish and, indeed, sometimes instructed to use it. Dr Ó Laoire's paper details some of the events in this process.

From the Spolsky and Ó Laoire papers, and the discussions resulting from them, it became quite clear how language revitalization is primarily an organic process that demands majority commitment to certain language behaviours rather than being primarily the business of state policy. Joshua Fishman has argued that intergenerational language transmission is the key process in any language maintenance or language revitalization process (Fishman, 1991).

This seemed to be the key difference between the two cases. In Israel, the proportion of Jewish settlers committed to switching the language of their family to Hebrew grew from an intellectual, middle class, educated, activist minority into a more widely based majority. In Ireland, this intellectual, middle class, educated, activist minority was not able to persuade the wider public to follow its example in speaking Irish within the home. The reasons advanced for this are complex: the Irish did not need to adopt a language that would unify a number of disparate speech communities; they possessed a vigorous and impressive Irish literary tradition expressed through the English language; they were used to accepting what Fishman has termed the state of being an 'Xman through Yish' (Fishman, 1991); the Catholic religion did not promote or require the use of the Irish language. Indeed the Catholic church was sometimes an actual opponent of the language revivalists. For example, the Catholic hierarchy bitterly opposed the 1913 law which required a matriculation in Irish for entrance to the Catholic university (Hindley, 1990). Thus we have, in Irish, the phenomenon of a threatened language with a state of its own, a state where it is the official language, a state where the education system promotes it, where entry into the state bureaucracies requires examination qualifications in it, where much of the national culture is expressed through it, and where its use is growing in the national media.

Professor Spolsky suggested that the decade before the first World War was the key period in which the multiple private decisions to switch language, made in the homes of the Jewish settlers in Palestine, established Hebrew as the language of the Jews in Palestine. The die was thus cast very early on in the twentieth century, and when the State of Israel was established, it was inevitable that Hebrew would be the language of the state. The multiple private processes were driven by the ambition of the modern (political) Zionists to see:

> an internally unified, culturally modernised and homogenised, 'reborn' people, in its old homeland (and) not only speaking its old language but speaking only its old language, insofar as its internal life was concerned. (Fishman, 1991: 7)

To achieve this it was, of course, necessary to displace Yiddish, the mother tongue of the vast majority of early settlers, and the language of the culturally dominant Eastern European group. The relentless campaign against Yiddish portrayed it as the language of the ghetto, the language of the victim, of the pogrom. The 'market repositioning' was successful. Yiddish did not remain a contestant as group language. Zionism would not tolerate Hebrew/Yiddish diglossia, with Hebrew for high functions and Yiddish for low. L-functions were reassigned to Hebrew, and Yiddish virtually disappeared. The events of the Second World War, which brought about intense group cohesion within the surviving Jewish community, untrammelled identification with Israel, and severed links with past homelands and languages served to complete the demise of Yiddish, and underpin the commitment to Hebrew.

The Zionist activists were mother tongue Yiddish speakers and had to go through the process of family language shift themselves. The English speaking Irish Republicans were in a similar situation but although many achieved language shift on the micro scale within their own families, they were not able to effect change on the macro-scale within the majority of Irish families.

The comparison between these two nations, both during their fight to establish a separate state and in their nation building strategies after achieving that aim, reveals much similar policy, many similar actions on the language front. However, the environments, the external pressures, the histories, the contribution of organised religion were each particular to the two cases and the linguistic outcomes have been, as a result, very different. The contrast between the success of Hebrew and the relative lack of success of Irish is illuminating The comparison is a reminder of the complexity of language planning. Effecting change in an area as profoundly personal as language use is neither easy nor predictable.

Note

1. The many schools of thought are well represented in the readings collected by John Hutchinson and A.D. Smith.

References

Fishman, J. (1991) *Reversing Language Shift*. Clevedon: Multilingual Matters.

Hindley, R. (1990) *The Death of the Irish Language*. London: Routledge.

Hutchinson, J. and Smith, A.D. (eds) (1994) *Nationalism*. Oxford: Oxford University Press.

Glinert, L. (1991) The 'back to the future' syndrome in language planning: The case of modern Hebrew. In D. Marshal (ed.) *Language Planning: Festschrift in Honor of Joshua A. Fishman*. Philadelphia: John Benjamin.

Obituary: Alexandra Korol

On April 13th 1996, Alexandra Korol died from cancer of the stomach. The diagnosis was late and at the time of the September 1995 meeting neither she nor we were aware of her illness.

Alexandra was born in West Ukraine, where she graduated and worked as a teacher. After the thaw in relations between Western Europe and the former Communist bloc, Alexandra came to Britain, to Manchester University, where she became a doctoral student working on the question of identity and ethnicity with particular relation to Ukrainians in Britain. She completed her doctorate successfully just before her death.

I first met Alexandra at a conference in Vienna before she came to the UK. She and I, like many in the early 1990s, were excited by the opening up of contacts between the East and West. We started corresponding. Her very bright intelligence, the insights that she brought from her early experiences, her irreverence and her charm made all contact with her a pleasure.

Once settled in Britain, Alexandra attended CILS seminars frequently. Those who met her there remember her with affection and admiration for her perception. It is with great sadness that we learned of her death and regret immensely the loss of a very attractive person and of the potential of a fine mind.

Sue Wright
Aston University
12th July 1996

Conditions for Language Revitalization: A Comparison of the Cases of Hebrew and Maori

Bernard Spolsky
Language Policy Research Center, Bar-Ilan University, Ramat-Gan 52900, Israel

Endangered Languages

In the summer of 1995, the European Network for Regional or Minority Languages and Education[1] reported that special courses were to be offered in Albanian, Aranese (Occitan in the Aran valley), Asturian (3), Basque (2), Breton (8), Catalan (4), Croatian (4), Dutch, Finnish (Tornedal, 5), Frisian (2), Gaelic (5), Irish Gaelic (5), Luxemburgish, Manx Gaelic, Romansch (various dialects, 5), Scottish Gaelic (5), Slovenian, and Welsh (8). These efforts at what Fishman (1991) has labelled Reversing Language Shift are one reaction to the realisation that many or most of the six thousand languages spoken in the world today are most likely to be extinct in the not too distant future.[2]

When attention was first focused on language loss by studies such as Joshua Fishman's optimistically named book *Language Loyalty in the United States* (1966),[3] the emphasis was on social changes of a language community. Two groups of linguists had more pessimistic views: philologists working to recreate 'dead' languages, either from scant surviving texts or by comparativist methods, and anthropological linguists carrying out fieldwork with the last speakers of a nearly extinct Native American language.[4] My own studies of Navajo[5] left me wondering if even a language with 120,000 speakers could stand up to the threat of spreading English, and this pessimism has been supported by developments in the past decade[6]. Of course, even a major world language like French can feel itself in danger, as witness recent policy attempts to defend it from the onslaught of English.

Language Death

The most tragic topic in the study of language shift is the death of a small language,[7] where we encounter, as Fishman (1989: 381) expresses it, the 'sorrows of the losers', 'their anguish, trauma and travail'. In contrast, the most joyous is the successful revival of one that had seemed moribund. Perhaps the strength of emotion felt by both participants and observers sometimes obscures a clear understanding of the nature of the phenomena.[8]

The belief in the merit of maintaining a multiplicity of languages, persuasively identified by Fishman (1982) as 'Whorfianism of the third kind',[9] does in fact provide a social consciousness, or even conscience, for linguists in general and sociolinguists in particular, without which the field would be both less humane and less responsible. Given the potential relevance of theory to practical problems being faced by speakers of an ailing language, the student of language shift is obliged to analyse and study the phenomenon with the utmost possible objectivity.

With all the problems involved in language maintenance, the most difficult is that concerned with control of the passing of a language from parents to children as a 'mother' tongue[10]. This phenomenon, labelled formally as 'intimate' or 'informal intergenerational transmission', is clearly the central feature of maintenance. If the chain is once broken, to repair it takes not just a major effort but, if not a miracle, then

> The rare and largely fortuitous co-occurrence of language-and-nationality ideology, disciplined collective will and sufficient societal dislocation from other competing influences to make possible a relatively *rapid and clean break with prior norms of verbal interaction*. (Fishman, 1991: 291; italics in original)

Language Revitalization

This paper deals with this kind of language restoration. To be more precise, it concerns a situation where people start again to use a language as the language of the home and in particular to speak it to newborn children after a period where these uses were extinct. It is one kind of language revival, it is best called *revitalization*.[11] It may be defined as the restoration of vitality (to use the term coined by Stewart (1968) to refer to use as a native language) to a language that had lost or was losing this attribute.

Language revitalization is a signal example of modifying the sociogeographic distribution and the functional allocation of language (Ferguson, 1983). It adds both a new set of speakers and a new function, spreading the language to babies and young children who become its native speakers. In this way, it assures intergenerational transmission, the crucial element in language vitality. At the same time, it adds the functions associated with the domain of home and family, resulting in various kinds of informal and intimate language use and the related emotional associations of the language.

I use the term revitalization rather than 'revival' which is misleading in cases such as Hebrew. As Cooper pointed out:[12]

> ... The term Hebrew revival is a misnomer. Hebrew is no exception to the rule that once a language has passed out of all use whatsoever, it remains dead. The 'revival' of Hebrew refers to its resuscitation as a vernacular, as a language of everyday spoken life. (Cooper, 1989: 19–20)

For in fact Hebrew remained alive, widely known and used for a wide range of important functions, throughout the centuries that followed its loss of native speakers. It is a mistake to confuse the terms and assume that revival and revitalization are the same thing. This lack of clarity about outcomes of language planning accounts for the widespread mistaken belief that, because it has not led to revitalization, Irish language revival has been a failure. As Dorian (1987) remarked, if one looks beyond the criterion of adding native speakers, Irish revival efforts have led both to an appreciable increase in the number of people who know the language and to a significant enhancement of its status.

In this paper,[13] my goal is to consider the specific conditions that seem best to account for Hebrew language revitalization. One aim will be to suggest a model of language revitalization that sorts necessary conditions from typicality ones. The detailed comparison I make with current efforts at Maori language revitalization[14] has three aims. The pragmatic aims is to help understand the process. The early stages of the revitalization process with Hebrew are no longer observable, and so looking at Maori offers a chance to see a process in operation.[15] The second is scientific, the need to have at least a second case to test the model. The third is the hope that this analysis of the Hebrew case will help those working on Maori language revival.

Models of Revitalization

In Spolsky (1991), I explored revitalization within a general model of second language learning. Language shift, loss, maintenance and spread, including revitalization, could usefully be seen, I proposed, as special cases of second language learning. While studies of second language learning generally concentrate their attention on the individual learner, the social phenomenon of language shift depends on groups of individuals who learn a language, who do not learn it, or who forget it. Thus what appears as a change in social patterns of language use and knowledge can be shown to depend on individual success or failure in language learning.

The general theory opportunities (Spolsky, 1989a: 15) proposes that language learning depends on previous knowledge, ability, motivation and learning. In the model, social context is relevant to language learning both in determining the attitudes and goals of the learner which lead to motivation, and in determining the learning opportunities, whether formal (e.g. educational) or informal, provided by those who interact linguistically with the learner.

I argued there that language revitalization depended fundamentally on the decision of parents or other significant caretakers to speak the moribund language to the young children in their charge; I suggested further that this decision was affected by a number of factors, some instrumental or pragmatic and some ideological or spiritual. I proposed that when there is conflict between the two kinds of factors, it takes particularly strong ideological force to overcome instrumental values.

The specific claim I presented was that the possibility of successful language revitalization was to be found partly in previous knowledge of the language by the adult sources, partly in the social factors which account for their attitudes and the children's attitudes, and partly in the resulting exposure of the children, in formal and informal circumstances, to the language. The level of knowledge on the part of the teachers or other sources of innovation have a strong effect: limitations in fluency or lexicon on the part of parents or teachers or other potential interlocutors, for instance, will hamper revitalization.

While there are many different social factors involved, both as causes of and as rationales for language revitalization, they may generally be grouped in two major categories, the pragmatic or instrumental on the one hand, and the ideological or integrative on the other. That is to say, one chooses to use a language because it is directly useful (economically, practically, for access to power or control) or because one values it for some social, cultural, nationalistic,

or religious reason. Successful language revitalization depends, it was hypothe-
sised, on establishing high enough solidarity value for the language being
revived to overcome any power or economic effects of the competing language.

Successful language revitalization also involves providing the learners with
sufficient exposure to the language, both in formal language teaching and in
informal language use, to make learning possible.

It is important to clarify the more restricted scope of my model from, for
instance, Kloss (1966), who set up a list of factors that might account for language
shift and language maintenance as a whole, or Fishman's (1991) concern on
efforts to reverse language shift. My focus is on informal intergenerational
language transmission, and not on some other form of transmission such as the
ethnoreligious transmission of Hebrew or the cultural-religious transmission of
Latin through formal educational systems. Nor am I concerned with the equally
important (and certainly much more common) efforts to raise the status of a
vernacular language to that of a standard language, even though the goal of such
an effort may be to lessen the chance of language shift taking place through lack
of motivation for informal intergenerational transmission.

My concern in this paper will be to isolate the conditions that appear necessary
or important to language revitalization, i.e. to encouraging new generations of
speakers (or even learners) of a language to speak it to their babies. To do this, I
wish first to clarify further both the temporal and the causative (or facilitative)
aspects of the process. This might help cast light on what is the crux of the whole
issue: understanding the point at which individual language learners feel
confident enough to rely on their new language. With Maori, it seems, the point
has not yet arrived. With Hebrew, I now suspect that the critical date was closer
to 1910 than to 1900. My first aim, then, is to the clarify the time chart for each
language revitalization programme.

The Ongoing Process of Maori Language Revitalization

Because I wish to use the Maori case,[16] which is still in progress and so open
to observation, to clarify and help resolve contradictions and confusions in the
records of the Hebrew case, I start with that.

As I described in an earlier paper,[17] the shift away from the use of Maori started
in the middle of the nineteenth century after the New Zealand land wars.[18] It may
be dated from the use of English as medium of instruction in Maori schools
starting in 1847, when the Education Ordinance subsidised mission schools on
condition that they taught in English, but the process of loss was at first slow.
The strength of Maori resistance in the New Zealand land wars, Belich (1986: 310)
argued, served to mitigate the effects of subjugation. The Maori people were able
to preserve their 'language, culture, and identity' providing a basis for the 'social
and political resurgence' that came later.

One early result of this resurgence was a Maori insistence that their language
be taught in secondary schools. There was continuing resistance to language loss
until the middle of this century, but eventually the pressure of using only English
from the earliest school years, and its growing use in the community, proved too
strong. Language loss was hastened when large numbers of Maori moved to the

cities. The effect was spread when some Maori moved back to the villages, bringing with them the city values that stressed the value of speaking English.

A sociolinguistic survey conducted by Richard Benton between 1973 and 1978 traced the process of Maori language loss.[19] In a town like Whangarei City, for instance, the erosion in ability to speak Maori was apparent as early as 1915; only 40% of Maori born there twenty years later could speak Maori; and most born after 1955 speak only English. Even in country areas, the switch to English seems to have begun in the 1930s, during the Depression, with certain areas moving much faster than others. As late as 1951, adult fluency in Maori could be taken for granted, and the 1951 census was accompanied by schedules printed in Maori. Material for teaching in Maori continued to be produced, but in the 1960s it was realised that few Maori children knew the language. By the time of Benton's survey, only two communities, Ruatoki and Matawaia, seemed to have maintained language vitality.

In the early 1970s, the final blow to continued language vitality may well have been the promotion of the use of English in the pre-school Play Centre movement, in which Maori mothers were urged to use only English with their children. This was reinforced by the spread of television. As a result, by the 1970s, the youngest native speakers of Maori were starting to grow older, there were no signs of a new generation of children growing up speaking the language, and the prospects for language survival were becoming dimmer. Looking at domains of language use, the picture was equally dismal. Only the *marae*, the site of traditional Maori *iwi* (tribal) activities, and some religious activities were clearly marked for Maori language use, and these too were showing signs of slippage.

By the late 1960s, Benton (1991) judges that 'Maori had ceased to be the primary language of socialisation for most Maori families'. In fewer than 8% of the households surveyed could the children understand Maori; in only half of these were the children considered fluent. It was not unreasonable then for Fishman *et al.* (1985: 45) to cite New Zealand and its Maori as a 'successful' case of 'translinguification', remarking that Maori ethnic identity seemed to be surviving the reported loss of the Maori language:

> The movement for revival and revitalization appeared in the early 1980s, supported externally by civil rights concerns associated with the anti-apartheid movement in New Zealand.[20]

Initial efforts to use elementary schools for the purpose of language revival appear not to have been successful:

> In the New Zealand situation, while the number of native Maori speakers has been progressively falling, government educational authorities and Maori leaders have sought to stage a revival in the school use of Maori. The children, however, are growing up in a predominantly English language world ... (Ritchie & Ritchie, 1979: 140)

The solution proposed to this impasse was to start teaching the children even before they went to school. A meeting of Maori leaders, sponsored by the Department of Maori Affairs in 1981, suggested the establishment of all Maori language pre-school groups, in which older Maoris, fluent speakers of the language, would conduct the programmes and make up for the fact that the majority of Maori parents could no longer speak their language. The first *kohanga reo* or language nest was set up in 1981. The Department of Maori Affairs provided encouragement and financial support, but the weight of organisation and implementation fell on the community that wanted one. Four experimental centres opened in 1982. Two years later, there were over 280 in existence; and by 1987 nearly five hundred centres,[21] under the aegis of the Kohanga Reo National Trust. The effect of the *kohanga reo* in exposing children to the language and its culture cannot be exaggerated. Fishman (1991) recognises the potential of this movement in reversing language shift of a language that was, before it started, virtually without child speakers.

The language revitalization process has also been boosted by political and legal pressure. A 1974 amendment to the Maori Affairs Act recognised Maori as 'the ancestral language of that portion of the population of New Zealand of Maori descent' but a number of court cases established, as Benton (1979) pointed out, that this had no practical meaning. However, in 1986, the Waitangi Tribunal held that the Crown had failed in its promise made in the Treaty of Waitangi[22] to protect the Maori language. It recommended (among other things) that Maori be made an official language, available as a language of instruction in schools, and watched over by a Maori Language Commission. Implementation began immediately. Maori was declared an official language of New Zealand and a Maori Language Commission,[23] was established. In addition, Maori started to be used as a language of instruction in some New Zealand schools, a move supported by parental pressure and recognised by the Department of Education.

My paper (Spolsky, 1989) surveyed the situation of Maori bilingual education in 1987. I noted three kinds of schools. There were a few older bilingual programmes, such as that at Ruatoki. There were a number of immersion programmes, none more than a year or two old, in which Maori-speaking teachers were exploring for the first time the presentation of a full syllabus. The third trend, of which two were in existence, were *kura kaupapa Maori* (Maori philosophy schools), independent of but funded by the Department,[24] where both instruction and curriculum are Maori.

The speed of development is shown in recent figures supplied by the Ministry of Education.[25] In 1990, there were six were *kura kaupapa Maori* serving 190 pupils; at the beginning of the 1995 school year, there were 38 catering for 3000 students. In addition, by 1993, 335 other schools offered some form of Maori medium instruction. In a third of these schools, Maori is being used 80% of the time. Thus, just over 1% of Maori children are in *kura kaupapa Maori*, and another 12.5% are receiving some other form of bilingual education. At the moment, the Ministry is undertaking a basic revision of the curriculum in mathematics, science and language. To meet the special needs of the Maori pupils, teams of Maori teachers are preparing and trying out separately developed Maori versions of the three draft curriculum statements.

To sum up the situation, we might first look at some figures. By the time of Benton's survey, only about 12% of adult Maori were speakers of the language. Over 55 years of age, the figure was closer to 50%; under ten years of age, there were only a handful of fluent speakers. Now, about 12% of younger children are on the way to a command of Maori; if they (and only they) succeed, there will have been success in reversing some 15–20 years of loss. Benton (1991) estimated that the *kohanga reo* movement was already producing some 3000 speakers a year; with the addition of the bilingual and immersion primary school programmes, and the continuation into secondary school programmes and beyond.[26]

But how successful has the reversal been? The numerical and political gains achieved in a few years have been remarkable, but Benton (1991: 30) warns against complacency: 'Tokenism in Maori language matters has often created an impressive facade of progress masking retrogressive reality'. He is particularly concerned about the draining of resources to teaching Maori language and culture to non-Maoris. The Ministry statistics for 1995 report that 93% of the children in Maori-medium education are Maori, but nearly half of the students studying Maori language at secondary school are not. Maoris make up only 18% of the 290,000 pupils who studied *Taha Maori* (a Maori culture programme) in 1993. These programmes that teach Maori as a New Zealand language rather than as an ethnically Maori one use up teaching resources that are sorely needed by the language revitalization programmes. In a press release for a speech earlier this year that was not in fact given, the Prime Minister, Mr Bolger, wrote that he was looking forward to the day when all New Zealand primary children would be comfortably bilingual in their two official languages. Even the most optimistic supporters of Maori revitalization suspect it will take some time before this is true even of ethnically Maori pupils.

For in truth, all signs are that the actual level of Maori knowledge and use remains quite low, even among students in immersion programmes. The difficulties of the switch cannot be denied. Most of the teachers involved in the *kohanga reo*, in the bilingual programmes, and in the *kura kaupapa Maori* are likely to be themselves second language speakers of Maori, with low fluency and restricted knowledge. At the same time, they are generally well educated in English. As a result, most use of the Maori language is restricted to the class-room. Even there, pupils regularly reply in English, and teachers often use English for more complex explanations. The children themselves continue to speak English both outside the class-room and with each other inside it. Only with their grand-parents is Maori likely to be fairly general.[27] Thus, the efforts have so far not led to the significant changes in language use that would count as successful revitalization. I will return to this question again later.

To summarise, I present a brief timeline for Maori language (see Table 1). In twenty years, educational programmes have been put in place that offer a chance of stemming language loss. It is premature to predict whether they will succeed, but useful to ask how the process to date matches the first stages of Hebrew revitalization.

The Process of Hebrew Language Revitalization

In this section I present a parallel description of the process of Hebrew language revitalization.

Although Hebrew ceased being a native language in daily spoken use,[28] it retained its place in most Jewish communities as a language to be read and to be written, to be prayed in and to be studied. It was used in secular domains as well:

Table 1

Year	Event
1814	First missionaries
1840	Treaty of Waitangi
1847	Anglicisation of schools starts
1920–35	Language loss at fast rate
1970–75	Language at low ebb, vitality almost nil
1981	*Kohanga reo* movement
1986	Maori language official; Maori Language Commission
1987	*480 kohanga reo*; a dozen bilingual schools, one or two *kura kaupapa* Maori
1990	*Six kura kaupapa Maori*
1995	38 *kura*, 335 other schools offering Maori medium instruction, 819 *kohanga reo.*

in writing legal, scientific, and philosophical texts, and, with the development of the Enlightenment, secular *belles-lettres*. An immense number of books were in fact written in Hebrew throughout this period when the language was not spoken. Hebrew thus continued to add new terms and to change to meet the demands of a changing world. It was far from a dead language.

At the same, time, there was restriction in its domains, serving mainly liturgical, scholarly and literary functions. Occasionally, it served as a lingua franca between Jews who had no other common language, but, as Harshav (1993: 107) remarks, the idea that there was extensive communication in nineteenth century Jerusalem between the established Ladino and Arabic-speaking Sephardic community and the newly arrived Yiddish-speaking Ashkenazim is a myth.

But it is also a mistake to assume that Hebrew before its revival was a language incapable of dealing with daily life. Glinert (1987) takes issue with the general 'Zionist-Hebraist' view represented by scholars such as Tur-Sinai and Avineri who made this claim, and which attributes the enrichment of the language to the work of secular scholars and committees in the early years of the twentieth century. Glinert produces evidence of a semi-vernacular religious Hebrew already available and in use. The forrn and resources of this variety can be judged from Ganzfried's Kitzur *Shulkhan Arukh*, an abridged and popularised guide to Jewish religious practice.[29]

The *Kitzur* was taught in the traditional Jewish elementary schools in Europe and in Palestine, and covered the daily life of a Jew, all aspects of which were fully governed by religious law. It required Hebrew words for such everyday items as fruit, vegetables and trees (some of which Avineri claims as later discoveries of the dictionary makers) as well as other normal objects of daily life. Because the first Hebrew teachers in the settlements had themselves had a religious education, they would have known these words.[30] Hebrew was a language with potential for modern use, and Jews with a solid education in it would have been ready to start trying to speak it.

Weinreich (1980: 311) points out that the revitalization of Hebrew involved a separation from the Diaspora and from the Yiddish that represented the Diaspora. At the same time, because of the complex pattern of functional allocation that existed between Yiddish and *lashon kodesh* (Fishman, 1976), the Hebrew speakers who were the pioneering speakers of modern Hebrew were able to draw on both Yiddish and *lashon kodesh* as they started to speak Hebrew as a vernacular daily language.[31]

The movement for Hebrew revernacularisation or revitalization[32] may be dated from the series of pogroms and repressive measures in Russia following the assassination of the Tsar Alexander II in 1881. These events started a wave of mass emigration of Jews. Some two million or so left Eastern Europe. Most of the emigrants found their way to America, but a small number came to Palestine, then a somewhat neglected outpost of the Ottoman Empire. Among them were young intellectuals, influenced by European nationalism, and imbued with the notion of building a life in Palestine that was better than and different from the one they had known in Eastern Europe. It was these Jews who started coming to Palestine in the 1880s who brought with them and embraced the notion of using Hebrew as their national language, an all-purpose vernacular that would serve to mark the distinction from life in the Diaspora.

The idea was first promulgated by Eliezer Ben-Yehuda, a young Russian Jew, who arrived in the Promised Land in 1881. He was an indefatigable promoter of the revival of Hebrew, in his prolific writing, in his speaking, and in his own practice: he was the first to insist on speaking Hebrew at home and to raise his own children speaking the language. Ben Yehuda himself lived in Jerusalem, but with a few distinguished exceptions, his arguments fell on deaf or even inimical ears, as the majority of the religious Jews in Jerusalem continued to favour the restriction of Hebrew to its sacred functions. It was to be in the new Zionist settlements that the revitalization of Hebrew was to take place.

In a discussion of Hebrew language revitalization Nahir (1988) proposes that there were four steps (or components, for they overlap) in what he calls the 'Great Leap' to Hebrew. First, the children of the community were 'instilled' with the required linguistic attitudes; second, they were presented with a model of language use in school; third, they themselves came to speak and use Hebrew not just in the school but also outside it, as a second language; fourth, when these children grew up, they started using Hebrew as the language of communication with their own children, who then grew up as native speakers.

The language learning model referred to above helps clarify the relations between these factors. Taking language use with children as the outcome, the necessary conditions are knowledge of the language on the part of teachers and parents, motivation of the teachers and parents to use the language, and the actual kind and amount of exposure. I have already mentioned the knowledge of Hebrew. In the next section, I will deal with the ideological basis for the decision taken to instill Hebrew in the children and to speak it. Here, then, my concern is with exposure.

How did the teaching actually start? Nahir says it followed from the decision to teach Hebrew in Hebrew, making use of the direct method. Until Eliezer Ben Yehuda's brief spell as a Hebrew teacher in Jerusalem in 1883, traditional European Jewish teaching had always assumed that Hebrew (and the Aramaic of the Talmud) was to be taught through Yiddish, the pupils' native language. Ben Yehuda taught, Fellman (1973: 49) reports, for a few months in an *Alliance Israèlite Universelle* school, using (at the suggestion of the principal, Nissim Bechar) the Berlitz (or direct) method of Hebrew through Hebrew.

In the schools of the agricultural settlements, under the patronage of the Baron de Rothschild, the regular medium of instruction for general subjects after 1884 had been French with Yiddish the language used for teaching Jewish subjects. There was no objection, however, when in 1886, David Yudelevic, emulated Ben Yehuda and started teaching Hebrew in Hebrew. Texts were prepared; all general subjects were taught in his school in Hebrew by 1888. By 1891, in several other colonies as well some subjects were being taught in Hebrew.

In 1892, a meeting of the nineteen members of the Hebrew Teachers Association decided that children of six should attend school for five years, that the Direct Method ('Hebrew in Hebrew') should be used, and that '... the explanation of the Bible is to be in Hebrew and in general all studies are to be explained in Hebrew' (Fellman, 1973). The next major step in providing children with opportunities to learn Hebrew was the opening of kindergartens, or preparatory programmes. In 1892 the Baron de Rothschild had opened a French kindergarten in Zikhron Ya'akov. Two years later, in 1894, a preparatory (pre-school) programme was opened in Rishon Le-Zion, in Hebrew, for four and five year-olds. The teachers were untrained; their work is reported to have been unimaginative. In 1896, three year-olds were admitted. A graduate of the school was sent to Jerusalem to be trained (at the Evelina de Rothschild school, in English). She returned in 1898 to open the first modern Hebrew kindergarten at Rishon Le-Zion with thirty pupils. More Hebrew kindergartens were opened, in Jerusalem (1903), in Safed, Jaffa, Haifa, Tiberias, Rehovot, Zikhron Ya'akov and Nes Ziyyonah (1904). Kindergartens became the main instrument of developing Hebrew fluency: 'Hebrew became almost the daily language of the youngsters' (Yosef Azaryahu cited by Fellman, 1973). 'The child became the teacher of his parents, his brothers, his sisters ...' (Chaim Zuta cited by Fellman, 1973).

A meeting of the Hebrew Teachers Association in 1895 adopted Hebrew as the language of instruction, with Sephardic pronunciation to be used (but Ashkenazic pronunciation was allowed in the first year in Ashkenazic schools, and for prayer and ritual). The next meeting of the association was not until 1903, at the close of a major convention of Jews of the Yishuv called in Zikhron Ya'akov by Ussishkin, the Russian Zionist leader. The fifty-nine members present accepted Hebrew as the medium of instruction of instruction and the direct method as the technique of instruction without much debate; there was general agreement also on the use of Ashkenazic script and Sephardic pronunciation.

The success of the new programmes in leading to language use was at first quite slow. Smilansky (1930) reports that in 1891 Hebrewschool graduates stopped speaking Hebrew when they left school. Harshav (1993: 87–8) points out the evidence for this. Many of the heroes of the revival confessed to the problems they had speaking the new tongue. Bialik (the premier Hebrew poet of the revival) and Eliezer Shteynman (another major literary figure of the revival) were reported to still converse in Yiddish in the 1930s. Yosef Klauzner, the first professor of Hebrew Literature at the Hebrew University confessed that he needed a French translation of the Hebrew book of Job to console him for his mother's death. Ben-Yehuda, in his autobiography, admitted to slipping — in his thoughts — into Yiddish, French or Russian.

Harshav (1993: 108) presents evidence on the slow progress. Ahad Haam reported on a visit in 1893 that both teachers and students stammered. Smilansky in 1891 reported that the speech of the 'fanatics' was 'artificial' and 'stammering'. A student in Rehovot Hebrew School in 1896 recalls that they spoke 'Hebrew with Yiddish'. The level of Hebrew instruction in the schools as late as 1900 is shown by the proposals made then for teaching elementary vocabulary. One textbook proposed teaching two to three hundred words. Yiddish and even French continued to be used in Zikhron Yaakov, more even than Hebrew, until well into the present century. Harshav concludes that the first twenty years or so of the revival were disappointing in their results. He cites a statement made by Shlomo Tsemakh in 1904:

> Many in Eretz-Israel know Hebrew, but very few, almost none, use it for everyday needs, and the question is how to turn those who know Hebrew into Hebrew speakers. (Translated and cited by Harshav, 1994: 109.)

The breakthrough came, Harshav proposes, with the Second Aliya (1904–14), a wave of better educated and highly ideological immigrants. In this period, only a small part of the hundreds of thousands of Jews who were leaving East Europe actually came to work in Israel.[33] The immigrants made up in ideological intensity for their small numbers: the slogan of *Ha-Poel Ha-Tzair* (the Young Worker movement) proclaimed in 1906 'Hebrew land, Hebrew work, and Hebrew language'. It was in these small groups, including people like David Ben-Gurion, Berl Katznelson, and Yitzhak Ben-Tzvi who became the leaders of the Zionist movement) that the first successful efforts were made to use Hebrew for daily life.

At the same time, there were two other critical developments. In 1899, Baron Rothschild ceased to be responsible for education in the Jewish settlements, and the way was left open for Hebrew to replace French, which probably happened by 1908. At this time, too, Hebrew was introduced to the city, especially in Tel Aviv, proclaimed from its beginning in 1906 as the 'first Hebrew city', with all its public business to be conducted in that language. The Hertzliya Gymnasium, a secondary school founded in Jaffa in 1906 and moved to Tel Aviv, and the Hebrew Gymnasium, founded in Jerusalem in 1908, were city high schools whose pupils learned in Hebrew and used it outside school.

The change to Hebrew use took place, then, between 1906 and 1914. Bachi (1956) reports that the 1916 census had 40% of Jews in Eretz-Israel (34,000 of 85,000) claiming Hebrew as their first or only language: the figures are higher

Table 2

Year	Event
1881	Eliezer ben Yehuda comes to Israel
1888–90	First Hebrew-medium schools in the settlements
1899	Rothschild leaves settlements
1906	Second Aliya, city schools
1913	Ezra schools switch to Hebrew

(75%) among the young.[34] The process of language revitalization, as I define it, then, took between twenty and twenty-five years, and while there remained a great deal to do to develop Hebrew as a full modern spoken and written language, the basis had been well established. A table summarising these events might be helpful (see Table 2).

Conditions for Successful Language Revitalization: A Preliminary Model

While the causes of language shift proved at first hard to sort out (Kloss, 1966), Fishman (1991) argues that (apart from obvious legal prohibitions on language use), the main reason seems to be dislocation of one kind or another. Physical and demographic dislocation are obvious. Physical dislocation is involved in immigration (as shown in the loss documented in the United States) or in urbanisation. Demographic dislocation refers to mixing of populations, as in the Soviet Union or in the Gaeltacht (O'Riagain). Social dislocation often results from physical or demographic dislocation, as bear witness the normally lower status of immigrants or higher status of colonists. Cultural dislocation is dangerous even — especially — when it is a consequence not of totalitarian oppression but of democratisation and modernisation. The traditional societies that maintained traditional languages were authoritarian and conservative.[35] The cultural changes associated with modernisation attacked both the traditions and the traditional language in which it was expressed.

For a language to have reached a situation where language revitalization is needed, where only a tiny proportion of intergenerational transmission is the result of home language use, one or more of the kinds of dislocation must have been operating. In principle, reversal of language shift would seem to require the use of the same force in an opposite direction. Physically or demographically, the language group needs to be returned to its original home or to its original demographic purity. Socially. the equality or superiority of the language group needs to be asserted or reasserted. Culturally, the traditional values and practices need to be restored or replaced by modified values or practices that can be shown or argued to derive from traditional values.

Various aspects of these relocations can be seen working in all the reversing language shift efforts described in Fishman (1991), and they are particularly important in the ideological bases for Hebrew and Maori revitalization.

The Ideological Basis for Hebrew Language Revitalization

From the end of Hebrew monolingualism, and certainly by the late Second Temple period, Jewish society tended to what Rabin (1981) labelled triglossia. The H language in this pattern, used for prayer and study and normally for all writing was *Lashon kodesh*, a blend of Hebrew and Aramaic. The L language, used within the home and the community in most other domains, was a Jewish language. Yiddish is the prototypical Jewish language, but there were many others: distinctively Jewish varieties of Aramaic, of Greek, of Spanish, of French, of Venetian and other Italian dialects, of Arabic, of Persian. Alongside these functioned a third language, the language used for dealing with the non-Jews, labelled by Weinreich (1980) as the co-territorial vernacular.

This triglossic background helps to make clearer what was involved in the ideologically motivated revitalization of Hebrew as part of the development of modern Jewish national identity. The unusual success of this revitalization owes much both to the continued role of Hebrew among Jews for the centuries when it was not spoken and to the strength of the ideological basis of the new movement.

Jewish emancipation in modern times set new choices both of identity and of language. In Western Europe, many Jews saw the possibility of assimilation of external values, combined with a rejection of both Hebrew and the Jewish languages. This may be seen with the development of the Reform movement. German was to be the language in which Jews expressed their religious identity. Their differences from Gentiles were to be theological but not linguistic or cultural. The use of the standard coterritorial language in the synagogue, itself renamed temple, marked an attempt at building a new identity.

The movement for the revival of Hebrew began in Eastern Europe and in Palestine in the latter part of the nineteenth century, under the influence of European national movements, which viewed the language of a people as inseparable from its nationhood. There was, however, as Rabin (1973: 69) noted, an essential difference between the Hebrew revival movement and the language movements associated with European nationalism. In the European cases, the usual task faced by the language revival campaign was to find a way to add literacy functions and formal status (H functions) to a spoken (L) variety of a language; in the case of Hebrew, the goal was opposite: to add spoken (L) functions to a language whose literacy status was already clearly established. Whereas the peoples mobilised by the European national movements could often be united by a common vernacular, the Jews were divided by their vernaculars, but they could be united by appeals to the symbolic association of Hebrew with tradition and peoplehood.

Emancipation offered the Western European Jews (transitorily, as it turned out) a chance to be reasonably like their non-Jewish neighbours, except in certain unexceptional religious tenets. The adoption of the standard language was the mark of this identity. Carried further, it offered a promise of complete assimilation.

The rise of nationalism in nineteenth century Europe made this easy assimilation difficult or impossible for many. The growth of the new national identities automatically marked Jews as outsiders. One response to this phenomenon was to develop a modern Jewish national identity. There were at least two distinct varieties of national identity offered, each associated with its own language. The first was the ultimately territorialist version of modern Jewish nationalism, called Zionism and associated with the revitalization of Hebrew. The second was the more culturally oriented version that adopted the standardisation of the Jewish vernacular, Yiddish, as its main emphasis.

These two movements and their associated language policies and practices have been well studied, so that I need touch on only a few features of each. The Zionist movement of the late nineteenth century was ideologically focused on the rejection of the artificiality (as it saw it) of Jewish life in the Diaspora. For Jews to regain their national identity, they needed the same things that other nations possessed: a land of their own, and their own language. While there was some wavering, the overwhelming sentiment was for return to the land from which Jews had been exiled eighteen hundred years before. It seemed logical to make the case that the new language of Jewish identity should be the language spoken before that dispersion, and in which the prayers for the return to Zion had been expressed daily ever since.

The attempts at language revitalization and at resettlement began independently — there were those who started to write and even speak Hebrew in Europe, and the early settlers in Palestine continued to use Yiddish for some years. But the process of revitalization took place both in the settlements where the Zionist pioneers were returning to the land as farmers and in the new Hebrew towns. There was important support for the process from ideologues and enthusiasts like Eliezer Ben Yehuda, but the revitalization itself depended on the those who had adopted the new identity of Hebrew farmers and townspeople in their historical Land. Their use of the revived language marked their own new identity.

An alternative approach was taken by proponents of Yiddish. Fishman (1980) has shown the importance of the 1907 Tshernovits conference in the development of the Yiddish nationalist movement. There were contradictory ideological winds blowing at that meeting. The Conference resolution, for instance, satisfied itself with proclaiming Yiddish as *a* Jewish national language, alongside Hebrew. One of the key organisers, Nathan Birnbaum, was a few years later to found what became the leading anti-Zionist religious party, *Agudat Israel*. Many of the people at the conference wrote in Hebrew as well as Yiddish. But the central theme was the value of developing a secular, nonterritorial, but decidedly Jewish cultural identity, to be expressed in Yiddish.

The Zionists were at the same time making their own decisions about language. In 1907 Po'ale Zion (a part of the Labour Party) issued two numbers of a periodical in Yiddish. This was strongly criticised by another faction, *Ha-Poel ha-Tzair*. The Labour party decided at the end of long debate in summer 1907 to issue its official journal only in Hebrew. It is significant that this decision was made one year before the Tsernovits conference, which Fishman (1980) holds as marking the establishment of an ideological basis for the Yiddish language movement; he (1980: 66) dates the proclamation of Yiddish as an expression and symbol of Jewish national identity to 1902–5. He also points out (1980: 69) that at Tsernovits it was possible to argue that because Zionists who favoured Hebrew had not rejected Yiddish, the conference in its turn should not reject Hebrew, and so the conference declared Yiddish *a* and not *the* national Jewish language.

It is important at this point to make clear the fundamental difference in the tasks undertaken by the proponents of the Yiddish revival movement and the Hebrew revival. For Yiddish, as with so many other European languages associated with national movements, the aim was to add or approve the addition of high status functions to a widely spoken but low status language; for Hebrew, the task was to add or approve the addition of daily use and speech (a low status function which could be raised ideologically) to a language with high status.

The dispute between the supporters of the two languages was marked by strong rhetoric and worse. In 1914, for instance, Chaim Zhitlowsky visited Palestine and lectured in Haifa, Jerusalem and Jaffa in Yiddish. The last of a planned series of lectures by him was disrupted by a demonstration of Herzliyyah high school pupils. Zhitlowsky in an article in *Ha-Ahdut* argued that only Yiddish could maintain the unity of the Jewish people. In a reply, A. Hashin argued that Yiddish was not revolutionary; only Hebrew could be the national language.

After the end of the First World War, supporters of Hebrew, concerned that new immigration from Europe would strengthen Yiddish, led a renewed ideological campaign. A proposal by N. Twerski that knowledge of Hebrew be a prerequisite for election to the autonomous Jewish institutions in Eretz-Israel was adopted at the Third Constituent Assembly of the Yishuv (new Jewish settlements in Palestine) in December 1918. At a meeting in Philadelphia of the American *Po'ale Zion* at the same time, a resolution was passed calling for equal rights for Yiddish in Palestine. The language question became a major issue in the struggle to unite the Labour movement. From 1925 until 1930, the debate in Palestine was much more personal, and attempts to found a chair of Yiddish at the Hebrew University in 1927 were defeated. The distinguished Hebrew poet, Nahman Bialik, who himself continued to speak Yiddish at home with his wife, was in the 1930s involved in a public incident with members of the self-styled Legion of Defenders of the Language. The struggle with Yiddish continued even after Hebrew was firmly established. It was seen as a continuing threat during the immigration of the early days of independence in the 1950s. Yiddish was the prototype enemy of Hebrew. It was the language associated with the Diaspora, and so of a rejected identity of Diaspora Jew. It was the language of the religious anti-Zionists, a group seen as a constant reminder of another rejected identity. And it was the language espoused by an ideology that had rejected territorialism and the return to Zion.

The struggles were bitter, vitriolic in rhetoric and from time to time moving to physical violence. As late as the 1970s, it was easy to find continuing evidence of the official persecution of the language (Fishman & Fishman, 1974). Yiddish could not, until quite recently, be admitted to schools and universities, or used on radio.[36]

The ideological choices offered to a young Jew growing up in say Odessa in the early years of this century were each tied to a language choice. If he chose to remain religiously observant, he would continue to speak his Yiddish mother tongue, study and write Hebrew all day, and learn the phrases of Ukrainian needed for dealing with his non-Jewish neighbours. If he were ready to attempt full assimilation — believing perhaps in the universalistic ideas of the new revolutionary socialist parties — he would feel bound to learn the local language. If he decided to follow the path of secular education, he would add to this a western language of science like German or French. And if he chose one or other version of Jewish nationalism, he would select either standardised and ennobled Yiddish or its rival, vernacularised and modernised revived Hebrew.

The beginning of Hebrew revitalization in these historical circumstances helps account for its ideological strength. The revitalization of Hebrew depended, I have argued, on this strong ideology. When Hebrew later spread to new immigrants, there was good instrumental motivation, as their acceptance in the new Hebrew-speaking society depended on their learning its language. But the settlements and towns where the language was revitalized between 1890 and 1910 were homogeneously Yiddish speaking, with no need for an internal lingua franca. Ideology was what counted.

Choosing Hebrew meant rejecting other languages. Arabic was perhaps not a serious choice, for while the Sephardim living in Safed and Tiberias and Jerusalem were fluent in the language, it was not the language of government. The Arabic used in Ottoman Palestine was a vernacular for street use, not a language for modern life. Turkish too was restricted to soldiers and senior officials.

French was a potential threat, partly because of its position as a high European language of culture, but more because it was the language of the Rothschild family who had supported the early agricultural settlements and their educational systems. Until 1899, secular education in the schools of the settlements was in French. Religious instruction was however in Yiddish, and at first, Hebrew was introduced for Jewish subjects and then, when the Baron's interests were turned elsewhere, for all subjects.

Another threat came from German, the language widely accepted at the beginning of the century as the language of advanced science and learning. The *Hilfsverein der Deutschen Juden*, established in 1901, worked to help the language spread policies of the German government. In the early years of the century, it established in Palestine a school system that ranged from kindergarten to teacher training college, which came to accept Hebrew as medium of instruction. It was the *Hilfsverein* that set off a furore in 1913 when its board proposed to establish a tertiary-level institute of technology in Haifa. This new institution was to use German as the language of instruction for science and technology. This proposal ignited the 'Language War', with pro-Hebrew teachers and pupils from the *Hilfsverein* joining in public demonstrations that led to the reversal of that decision.

Rejecting these languages and choosing Hebrew was also rejecting ideologies associated with them, for as Harshav (1993: 92) makes eminently clear, the proponents of Hebrew revitalization saw themselves as establishing not just a new language but also a new society. 'It was', he points out, 'a revival not only of the Hebrew *language* but also of Hebrew *culture* and a Hebrew *society'*. They set out to establish a new way of life in a new country. From the commercial life of the East European *shtetl*, they turned to life as farmers (the First Aliya) or, even more radically, to life in communal settlements.

> A handful of young people in strange landscapes, in a desolate and hostile world, the first generation of a budding society, a society without parents and grandparents, they surrounded their precarious existence with a brand-new fence — a fence of an emotionally perceived ideology and a new Hebrew language. (Harshav 1993: 9)

Those who planned to build cities planned that the cities would be Hebrew-speaking and clean:

> We must urgently acquire a considerable chunk of land, on which we shall build our houses. Its place must be near Jaffa, and it will form the first Hebrew city, its inhabitants will be Hebrews a hundred percent; Hebrew will be spoken in this city, purity and cleanliness will be kept, and we shall not go in the ways of the goyim. (1906 Prospectus for Tel Aviv, cited and translated in Harshav 1993: 143)

In rejecting other languages, the proponents of Hebrew were rejecting other ways of life as well:

> The revival of the Yishuv, the new Jewish community in Eretz-Israel, was also formulated to a large extent in contrasting oppositions: Zionism as opposed to a Socialist solution in the Diaspora; Hebrew as opposed to Diaspora Yiddish; the 'Sephardi accent' as a 'pioneer' and 'masculine' language as opposed to the 'moaning' and religious Ashkenazi Hebrew; a 'Hebrew' people and 'Hebrew' work as opposed to the distorted 'Jewish' character … (Harshav, 1993: 21)

It was the force of these ideologies, strong enough to bring those who held them to a 'hostile and desolate world' that accounted for the strength of motivation to adopt a new language from within. Of the two million or so Jews who left Eastern Europe between 1882 and 1914, only a select and highly motivated group chose Eretz-Israel, and many of them left before or during the First World War. For those who moved to the West, or for those others who left the *shtetl* for the cities, the switch from Yiddish to the co-territorial vernacular was largely the normal acculturation of immigrants to the instrumental claims of the receiving society. For the tiny group who came to Palestine, there was no instrumental push to adopt the language of the surroundings, but a much more difficult task to develop and revitalize a language. They accepted physical dislocation, but found a way to relocate demographically, socially and culturally. The result was successful language revitalization. It took some forty years, but by 1921, Hebrew, changed as it was in the process, was once again a living language.

The Ethnic and Ideological Basis for Maori Language Revitalization Efforts

Looked at from outside, the Maori revival efforts appear to be simply a part of a politically and economically motivated ethnic movement. There is no denying that Maori people are economically, educationally and culturally disadvantaged. They have moved to the cities (physical and demographic dislocation) forming a large and worrisome underclass, with high levels of unemployment, suicide, drunkenness and crime (social dislocation) and given up on much of their traditional language, culture, and way of life (cultural dislocation).

The language revitalization programmes can be seen — as the Ministry clearly does — as simply a way of dealing with the social problem, by improving retention at school and trying to catch up with the still widening gap between Maori and non-Maori education. The economic aspects of the other Waitangi Tribunal activities are also salient, with conflict imminent about the enormous cost of meeting claims for lands seized contrary to the terms of the Treaty.[37] The claim for Maori language restoration look as much like an economic matter as do the claim for restoring fishing rights or the claims for access to public radio and television channels.

If no more than this is involved, there is the possibility that meeting the political or economic claims will lead to a loss of interest in language matters. One is reminded of what happened with Navajo education. The initial campaign in the early 1970s for Navajo control of schools on the Reservation was language related. During the 1970s, the Tribe gained increasing control of the schools, and over a 1000 Navajo teachers were trained and appointed. With a handful of exceptions, these schools and teachers use English, and Navajo language loss is proceeding at an increasing pace.

The question, then, is the strength and nature of ideological support for the language revitalization movement. Does it go beyond the linguistic, the economic and the social spheres? Are there signs of the strength of ideology, of the cultural motivation, that will lead educated Maori native speakers of English to shift to their less well controlled Maori?

There are hints of this. First, the *Kohanga reo* movement was community based and has constantly shied away from too cosy a relationship with government. Only now, fourteen years after the movement started, has a university-based training programme been started for all Maori immersion early childhood teachers,[38] complementing the Whakapakari programme operated by the Kohanga Reo Trust. In developing the curriculum, the need for Maori control was asserted:

> It is therefore important that Maori retain control of programme design and development, are at the centre of gathering a knowledge base and are responsible for programme implementation. (Ritchie, 1994: 4)

Both the *kohanga reo* and the bilingual and immersion programmes within public schools have been concerned with maintaining ethnic identity. In my earlier paper, I described the ceremonies I went through to enter the immersion classrooms. I cite that description:

I mentioned the formal *powhiri* or welcome at Wilford School, but it was on the trip to the Waikato and East Coast that I really started to learn protocol. My escort (a Maori education adviser) had told me that we would be met by some of his colleagues who would look after us, and while we were sitting talking to the newly appointed Maori principal and his Maori school committee chairman at Rakaumunga School, four women (education advisers and itinerant teachers of Maori) arrived to fill an important role in the ceremony.

The greeting ceremony in the Waikato and East Coast generally followed the same pattern. Our party would wait, in a staff-room or principal's office or at the school gate, for a signal that it was time to enter. Preceded by one of the women with us, we would then walk in procession towards the classroom or building where the greeting was to take place. A local woman (a teacher or a pupil), would then appear and sing the *karanga*, to which our escort would reply. We would enter the room and sit down on a row of chairs. Facing us would be the school, or the class, with at least two men (teachers or school committee members) on their right. The *powhiri* started with a speech in Maori from the senior (in Maori terms) local person — sometimes the school principal or deputy principal, or school board chairman. At the end of the speech (which lasted about five minutes), the school would stand and sing a *waiata*. After a second speech of welcome and *waiata*, the male education adviser escorting me would give the first reply, after which the visiting group would stand and sing its *waiata*. I gave the second reply, starting my speech (at the suggestion of my escort) in Hebrew and then going on to explain (in English) something about Hebrew language revival.

After a *waiata*, we would hand over an envelope containing money as a substitute for the offering of food that is a traditional part of the visitor's role. The *powhiri* would conclude with the visiting party moving along a row of the local group (the adults and a few of the children) in order to shake hands and press noses.

It took me a while to grasp the significance of these formal Maori receptions that preceded most of my visits. In Wilford, it had seemed like a rather charming display of Maori culture, but on the Waikato and East Coast trip I came to appreciate that it served a number of important functions. In part, of course, there was the traditional Maori concern for showing respect to a visitor. One important aspect of this was the reciprocal effect. The more impressive the ceremony, the more important the visitor; but the more important the visitor, the more important the place he has chosen to visit. The showing of respect to an international expert in bilingual education showed in its turn the importance ascribed by the Department of Education to the particular programmes I was taken to visit. The ceremonial then had a positive value for the local community, and served to proclaim the importance of the bilingual programme.

The second interesting function performed by the traditional ceremony was its definition and underlining of the Maoriness of the bilingual programmes I visited. The *powhiri* is the ceremony performed when guests come to a marae-atea, the physical space designated by a Maori group for traditional formal activities. One might consider the analogy of the sign found in many American schools that says 'Visitors must report to the Principal's Office'. The purpose of the sign is to make clear that access to the school is through the administrative bureaucracy; like the special badges given to visitors to a building with special security, they determine the degree of access allowed. These traditional Maori ceremonies made clear that access to the bilingual programme is under traditional Maori community control: the decision to admit a visitor is made not in an administrative but in a traditional way; visitors report not to the principal but to the local Maori community, and are clearly labelled as visitors. This was brought home to me by the remark of one European school principal, as I was leaving after a morning spent in his school's bilingual programme, that he has a policy requiring visitors to spend at least three days and look as the school as a whole; I interpreted this as an explanation of how my formal welcome by the *whanau* had replaced his regulation.

The establishment of the Maori bilingual programmes as Maori space was also emphasised by the physical surroundings; the classrooms were decorated with Maori art, and a number had traditional carvings in them as well. Thus, the bilingual programmes are establishing physical and social space for the process of linguistic and cultural revival. The schools I visited were state schools, but they had found ways, in the use of Maori as sole language of instruction and in other symbolic ways, to declare Maori space, a move towards the possible establishment of *Kaupapa Maori* schools, schools with a complete Maori philosophy. (Spolsky, 1989)

The *kura kaupapa Maori* are the third of the signs of ethnicity, revolutionary proclamations of opting out not just linguistically and ethnically but also ideologically from the mainstream. The terminology of the *kura* is Maori. It incorporates *Tikanga Whakaako* (Maori pedagogy), which uses culturally pre-ferred methods and *Te Reo* (the Maori language) based on *Tikanga* (the ethical basis of Maori philosophy and practice) to teach *Taonga Tukuiho* (cultural aspirations principle), with full emphasis on the past, in order to assure *whakapapa* (intergenerational continuity) for the *whanau* (family and community).[39]

The rapid expansion of the *kura kaupapa Maori* over the past few years has been facilitated by the reform in the New Zealand educational system introduced in the closing years of the Labour Government. Under this Thatcherite scheme, regional school boards were abolished, and each individual school was required to set a board to negotiate a charter directly with the Ministry. The National Government has continued this policy, which makes provision for Government funding of approved non-public schools. Under this provision, the present Minister has approved sixteen new *kura kaupapa Maori*, and changed nine other schools to the status.

These three initiatives show the leaders of the Maori revitalization movement both opting out of the mainstream and working for the maintenance of *Te Reo*

Maori as a critical method of re-establishing the *whanau* (family) and iwi (tribe). The social and cultural relocation are being combined with physical and demographic relocation. While there has perhaps not been a great deal of return to the traditional village, there has been the building of Maori space in the cities, both in the new *maraes* and in the defined educational space of *kohanga reo*, immersion programme, and *kura kaupapa Maori*.

Maori and Hebrew: Contrasts and Similarities[40]

The comparison of Maori and Hebrew revitalization efforts is especially illuminating for the light it casts on the phenomenon of ideological revitalization. It is of course important to recognise the major differences, and I do this at the outset. The situation of the two languages at the beginning of the process was quite different: Hebrew had been unused as a spoken language for some 1700 years, while Maori still had significant numbers of older native speakers alive (see Table 3).

With its long literary tradition, Hebrew had the potency of a language with an immense storehouse of written material that recorded the constant shaping of the language to changing intellectual and practical needs. Maori depended on

Table 3

Stage	Hebrew	
	Year	Event
Language Loss	100 BCE	Bilingualism.
	200 CE	Loss of vitality.
Revitalization efforts	1881	Eliezer ben Yehuda comes to Israel.
	1888–90	First Hebrew-medium schools in the settlements.
Fluent use	1906	Second Aliya, city schools.
and vitality	1913	Ezra schools switch to Hebrew.

Stage	Maori	
	Date	Event
Language loss	1900	Bilingualism.
	1960	Loss of vitality.
Revitalization efforts	1981	*Kohanga reo* movement starts.
	1986	Maori official; Language Commission bilingual schools.
	1987	480 *kohanga reo*; a dozen bilingual schools; one or two *kura kaupapa Maori*.
	1990	Six *kura kaupapa Maori*.
	1993	38 *kura*, 335 other schools offering Maori-medium instruction.

an oral tradition, good parts of which were recorded in writing in the nineteenth century, and on a period of adaptive literacy during the second half of the nineteenth century.

There was also a major difference in the changes involved. Hebrew had the task of adding an L variety to an H language. That is to say, the process of revitalization was at the same time one of vernacularisation. For Maori, the task was adding modern H functions to a language restricted in its domains. The tasks then is standardisation.[41] Allowing for these and other differences, the similarities remain notable. The first was the initial attempt to make the transition by gaining control of the school system, and when that seemed insufficient, by adding a pre-school component. The second was the independence of government initiative. The Hebrew and Maori efforts were neither of them the result of a government planning decision, but rather the activity of minority ethnic-based ideologies working to establish new identities. Both had to deal with physical, demographic, social and cultural dislocation.

Hebrew has succeeded in its goals, although the results have turned out somewhat differently from what was envisaged. Certainly there are complaints voiced by normativists that the language has changed unrecognisably.[42] And there are concerns expressed about the future vitality of the language, but they are no more than are found with most languages in the world today threatened by English.

For Maori, the issue is undecided as yet. Language revitalization efforts have reached the critical state, perhaps a little faster than with Hebrew, where the important breakthrough into vernacular fluency followed by *whakapapa* (normal intergenerational transmission) is still a challenge.

Notes

1. In MERCATOR-EDUCATION, issued by the Fryske Academy, April 1995.
2. Krauss (1991) is one of the first papers to make this point.
3. Fishman usually prefers positive titles: *Advances ...*, *Progress ...*, *Spread ...*, etc. Although it is true that lately he has acknowledged *The Rise and Fall of the Ethnic Revival* and the need for *Reversing Language Shift*.
4. Spolsky & Kari (1978) for instance, while talking about language maintenance, trace the gradual loss and extinction of the Athapaskan language.
5. Summed up in Spolsky (1975).
6. Fishman (1991: 189–90) reports that 'the slow shift to English is now noticeable even in Reservation-interior communities'.
7. Dorian (1981) shows what can be learned about the process of language death.
8. It is not surprising that the study of minority languages is largely a-theoretical, as scholars' feelings of regret or triumph, cloud or brighten their perception of the object of their study, and of the forces working on it. This said, I am not sure that I would like the situation to be very different: dispassionate scholarship is possible only from a valueless position and easily serves to justify the absence of concern for the people whose fate is being studied. For a moving presentation of this point, see the author's preface to Fishman (1991).
9. For a fuller discussion of reasons to attempt to maintain threatened languages, see Fishman (1991: especially Chapter 3) who stresses the ethnocultural value, and Krauss (1991) who stresses the need to maintain differentiation in human species.
10. Haugen (1991) shows that the term was originally pejorative: fathers could teach Latin, but mothers could only pass on the vernacular, but by the time of Dante, it had acquired more elevated and less chauvinistic usage.

11. Fishman (1991) uses the term *revernacularisation* specifically referring to cases like Hebrew, where the vernacular was added to a classical language.
12. In this statement he was agreeing with Fellman (1973, 1974) and Rabin (1973).
13. This paper revises in a number of significant ways the model and claims presented in Spolsky (1991) and in Spolsky and Cooper (1991).
14. In doing this, I will be updating information and tentative conclusions in Spolsky (1989b).
15. Inability to observe the process with Hebrew, and difficulties in interpreting contemporary descriptions have led some scholars to give up on the 'examination of the problematic evidence and investigation of every person who spoke or taught Hebrew (the accounts of which are not clear anyway)', as Harshav (1993) confessed.
16. Other cases that might be equally revealing are Basque and Frisian.
17. Spolsky (1989b) was based on a study carried out at the request of the New Zealand Ministry of Education. The recommendations of the study are remembered, but have yet to be implemented.
18. A series of armed struggles between Maori *iwi* and British settlers and soldiers, lasting until the late 1800s.
19. While the full details of this report remain unpublished, the most recent analysis provided by Benton (1991) supplies the basis for this summary.
20. Graeme Kennedy (personal communication) suggested this to me.
21. Ritchie (1994) reports that 49% of the Maori children enrolled in early childhood services (some 46% of Maori children under the age of 5) are in *kohanga reo*. The Ministry of Education reported that Maori enrolment in early childhood coeducation doubled between 1983 and 1993.
22. In this Treaty, signed in 1840, Britain asserted sovereignty, with the undertaking that Maori land and other rights would be protected. The Tribunal rules that language was one of the protected rights.
23. *Te Komihana mo te Reo Maori*, chaired by Professor Timoti S. Karetu.
24. It is significant that *kura kaupapa Maori* is the first language initiative mentioned in the 1994 Ministry Report on the Ten Point Plan for Maori education.
25. In a document entitled *Maori Educational Trends* dated January 1995. My thanks to Rawiri Brell, Group Manager Maori in the Ministry of Education for these data and for comments on an earlier version of this paper.
26. The Ministry reported the existence of two *wananga* or Maori tertiary institutions, with 281 full-time equivalent places for 1994 and 473 places promised for 1995. These two Maori universities are in addition to Maori programmes in mainstream universities and in teacher training institutions. Maoris make up 8% of university students, 11% of polytechnic students, and 10% of college of education students.
27. In my 1987 visit, and again during discussions in 1995, I asked if there was evidence yet of informal use of Maori by pupils outside school. There was not, and the people I spoke too (active as teachers of Maori) confessed that they found it difficult to keep up Maori with their children at home. I observed English being used by Maori children in a *kohanga reo* especially when they were addressing the adults who were their own parents.
28. The date of this is disputed. Rabin has suggested that the last monolingual speaker would have been at the time of the Bar Kokhba Revolt (c. 120 CE); Fraade (1990) believes that Hebrew was still being spoken as a daily language in the Galilee as late as the 6th Century.
29. First published in Hebrew in Hungary in 1864. By 1908, more than twelve editions — 400–500,000 copies — had appeared, including plagiarised ones.
30. Fellman (1973: 51) cites the account of one of these early teachers, Yizhaq Epstein, who claims to have had little Hebrew education beyond elementary school; but this included Talmud until he entered High School, after which he read 'very little' modern Hebrew literature.
31. It would be ironic if continued research were to establish that the contemporary Hebrew language owes its basic Indo-European bent to the Yiddish with which it successfully competed for loyalty.

32. To distinguish it from the earlier cultural revival associated with the *Haskala*.
33. Harshav (1994: 135) cites an estimate that the number of immigrant workers in this period was not more than 3000.
34. Harshav (1994: 111–12) is doubtful of these numbers.
35. Consider for instance the place of women in most of them.
36. But things have changed in the last decade or so: see for instance, Hallel & Spolsky (1993).
37. The demonstration that prevented the Prime Minister making his speech about his commitment to bilingualism was aimed at a proposal by the government to set a cap on the amount of compensation to be paid on all outstanding claims under the Treaty of Waitangi.
38. It is significant that this initiative began under the aegis of the Maori-controlled *Te Puni Kokiri* (Ministry of Maori Development) but has now moved to the Ministry of Education.
39. The terms and their translations are taken from Appendix 1 to Ritchie (1994).
40. It is intriguing that one of the important assignments in a course on language revitalization, as part of the programme for training Maori early childhood teachers, is to compare the Maori and Hebrew cases. See Appendix V to Ritchie (1994).
41. Both also involved modernisation.
42. Both the Hebrew Language Academy and the Maori Language Commission express these concerns regularly.

References

Bachi, R. (1956) A statistical analysis of the revival of Hebrew in Israel. *Scripta Hierosolymitana* 2, 179–247.
Belich, J. (1986) *The New Zealand Wars and the Victorian Interpretation of Racial Conflict*. Auckland: Auckland University Press.
Benton, Richard A. (1979) *The Legal Status of the Maori Language: Current Reality and Future Prospects*. Wellington: Maori Unit, New Zealand Council for Educational Research.
Benton, Richard A. (1991) The Maori language: Dying or reviving. Working paper prepared for the EastWest Center Alumni-in-Residence Working Papers Series.
Cooper, Robert L. (1989) *Language Planning and Social Change*. Cambridge: Cambridge University Press.
Dorian, Nancy (1981) *Language Death: The Life Cycle of a Scottish Gaelic Dialect*. Philadelphia: University of Pennsylvania Press.
Dorian, Nancy (1987) The value of language maintenance efforts which are unlikely to succeed. *International Journal for the Sociology of Language*, 68, 57–67.
Fellman, Jack (1973) Concerning the 'revival' of the Hebrew language. *Anthropological Linguistics* 15, 250–7.
— (1974) *The Revival of a Classical Tongue: Eliezer Ben Yehuda and the Modern Hebrew Language*. The Hague: Mouton.
Ferguson, Charles A. (1983) Language planning and language change. In Juan Cobarrubias and Joshua A. Fishman (eds) *Progress in Language Planning: International Perspectives* (pp. 29–40). Berlin: Mouton.
Fishman, Joshua A. (1976) Yiddish and Loshn-Koydesh in traditional Ashkenaz: Problems of societal allocation of macro-functions. In Albert Verdoodt and Rolf Kjolseth (eds) *Language in Sociology* (pp. 39–489). Louvain: Editions Peeters.
— (1980) Attracting a following to high-culture functions for a language of everyday life: The role of the Tshernovits Conference in the 'Rise of Yiddish'. *International Journal for the Sociology of Language* 24, 43–73.
— (1982) Whorfianism of the third kind: Ethnolinguistic diversity as a world-wide societal asset. *Language in Society* 11, 1–14.
— (1989) Language spread and language policy for endangered languages. In Joshua A. Fishman (ed.) *Language and Ethnicity in Minority Sociolinguistic Perspective*. Clevedon: Multilingual Matters.
— (1991) *Reversing Language Shift*. Clevedon: Multilingual Matters.
Fishman, Joshua A. and Fishman, David E. (1974) Yiddish in Israel: A case study of efforts

to revise a monocentric language policy. *International Journal of the Sociology of Language* 1, 126–46.

Fishman, Joshua A., Gertner, M.H. Lowy, E.G. and Milan, W.G. (1985) *The Rise and Fall of the Ethnic Revival: Perspectives on Language and Ethnicity.* Berlin: Mouton.

Fishman, Joshua A., Vladimir Nahimy, John Hofman, Robert Hayden *et al.* (1966) *Language Loyalty in the United States.* The Hague: Mouton.

Glinert, Lewis (1987) Hebrew-Yiddish diglossia: Type and stereotype implications of the language of Ganzfried's Kitzur. *International Journal of the Sociology of Language* 67, 39–56.

Hallel, Michael and Bernard Spolsky (1993) The teaching of additional languages in Israel. *Annual Review of Applied Linguistics* 13, 37–49.

Harshav, Benjamin (1993) *Language in Time of Revolution.* Berkeley: University of California.

Haugen, Einar (1991) The 'mother tongue'. In Robert L. Cooper and Bernard Spolsky (eds) *The Influence of Language on Culture and Thought: Essays in Honor of the 65th Birthday of Joshua A. Fishman* (pp. 75–84). Berlin: Mouton.

Kloss, H. (1966) German-American language maintenance efforts. In Joshua A. Fishman *et al.* (eds) *Language Loyalty in the United States.* The Hague: Mouton.

Krauss, Michael (1991) The world's languages in crisis. *Language* 68 (1), 4–10.

Nahir, Moshe (1988) Language planning and language acquisition: The 'Great Leap' in the Hebrew revival. In Christina Bratt Paulston (ed.) *International Handbook of Bilingualism and Bilingual Education* (pp. 275–95). New York: Greenwood Press.

Rabin, Chaim (1973) *A Short History of the Jewish Language.* Jerusalem: The Jewish Agency.

— (1981) What constitutes a Jewish language. *International Journal for the Sociology of Language* 30: 19–28.

Ritchie, James and Jane Ritchie (1979) *Growing Up in Polynesia.* Sydney: George Allen and Unwin.

Ritchie, Jenny (1994) Development of Maori immersion early childhood education. Paper read at the International Language Conference, University of Hong Kong, December 14–16, 1994.

Smilansky, Ze'ev (1930) Letoldot hadibur ha'ivri be'eretz yisrael. (Towards a history of spoken Hebrew in Palestine). *Hapo'el Hatsa'ir* 23, 7.

Spolsky, Bernard (1975) Prospects for the survival of the Navajo language. In M. Dale Kinkade, Kenneth Hale and Oswald Werner (eds) *Linguistics and Anthropology, in Honor of C.F. Voegelin* (pp.597–606). Lisse: The Peter de Ridder Press.

— (1989a) *Conditions for Second Language Learning: Introduction to a General Theory.* Oxford: Oxford University Press.

— (1989b) Maori bilingual education and language revitalization. *Journal of Multilingual and Multicultural Development* 9 (6), 1–18.

— (1991) Hebrew language revitalization within a general theory of second language learning. In Robert L. Cooper and Bernard Spolsky (eds) *The Influence of Language on Culture and Thought: Essays in Honor of the 65th Birthday of Joshua A. Fishman* (pp. 137–55. Berlin: Mouton.

Spolsky, Bernard and Robert L, Cooper (1991) *The Languages of Jerusalem.* Oxford: Clarendon Press.

Spolsky, Bernard and James Kari (1978) Trends in the study of Athapaskan language maintenance and bilingualism. In Joshua A. Fishman (ed.) *Advances in the Study of Societal Multilingualism* (pp. 635–664). The Hague: Mouton.

Stewart, William (1968) A sociolinguistic typology for describing national multilingualism. In Joshua A. Fishman (ed.) *Readings in the Sociology of Language* (pp. 531–545). The Hague: Mouton.

Tsemakh, Shlomo (1965) *The First Year.* In Hebrew, Tel Aviv: Am Oved.

Waitangi Tribunal (1986) Findings of the Waitangi Tribunal relating to *Te Reo Maori* and a claim lodged by Huirangi Waikarapuru and *Nga Kaiwhakapumau i te Reo* Incorporated Society (The Wellington Board of Maori Language), issued April 29, 1986.

Weinreich, Max (1980) *History of the Yiddish Language* (translated by Joshua A. Fishman and Shlomo Noble). Chicago: University of Chicago Press.

The Debate

Building a Model: Extrapolating from the Hebrew and Maori Experience

Bernard Spolsky (Bar-Ilan University): This paper was written while I was engaged in practical language policy development, so I think it useful to give some background. Before 1995, Israel had no explicit policy on language education, although there were some elements of such a policy in place. My colleague, Professor Elana Shohamy of Tel Aviv University, and I suggested to the Ministry of Education that there should be a single document setting out language education policy. We were asked to prepare a draft position paper, and the Language Policy Research Center at Bar-Ilan University was awarded a three-year grant to work on issues related to language education policy. In our early drafts, we were cautious because of the complex political, social, ethnic, religious, and cultural issues that surround the subject.

The Israeli Ministry of Education has to set policy on a number of matters involving language. The first is the question of language of instruction. In State Schools in the Jewish sector, the language of instruction is Hebrew. In State Schools in the Arab sector (some 19% of pupils), it is Arabic. There is provision for the compulsory teaching of Hebrew in the Arab schools, and for the compulsory teaching of Arabic in the Jewish schools. In both systems, English is taught compulsorily as the principal foreign language. Other languages with significant numbers of students are French, Russian and Yiddish.

One of the issues that worried us most was the continued ideological status of Hebrew; there was an incident about a year ago when a proposal came up in the Ministry of Education to try to teach English a little bit more intensively in some classes. There is a very big demand in Israel for English and at the moment the official policy says that students will learn English from the fifth to the twelfth grade. Universities all require an exam in English for admission, although the medium for teaching at university level is Hebrew. Nonetheless, all disciplines assume that a university student needs to be able to read English. In practice, the students know how to get through university without being able to read English but the professors still believe that they have to be able to read English — a difference between what people think is happening and what actually happens.

Given this and given the status of English as a world language, the fact that people who do better economically know English and those that are striving for a better economic position think it would be very good for their children to know English, there is a buoyant demand for the teaching of that language. As I already said, the official policy requires English from the fifth grade but more and more parents have been requesting English as early as the third grade. In fact in larger cities like Tel Aviv we think that 80% of the children do start in the third grade, so that there is widescale disregard for the actual policy; funds are found in a variety of ways to make sure this demand is met. In our studies, we are noting that there is now increasing demand for even younger children to be instructed in English. It is interesting that the demand for first and second grade teaching for English is particularly strong in the Arab sector.

Now, as part of that pressure to teach English, a proposal was made to do what we would call teaching language through context. The proposal was based on the model that Michael Clyne presents in the teaching of German in Melbourne where you teach a few subjects, the content of which is obvious like music, physical education, etc., in the language. The proposal was to take a total of nine experimental schools and let them teach one or two extra hours a week in their chosen content area. The people who were making the proposal used the term immersion, because immersion is a very acceptable word these days when trying to teach languages and this was the word picked up by the newspapers in their reports of our plans to start 'immersion' teaching of English in the first and second grades.

The Hebrew Language Academy immediately called a meeting and invited the Minister of Education to come to the meeting. They expressed sheer horror at the threat to 'kill' Hebrew by this massive immersion teaching of English; the Minister who probably wasn't very well instructed in all the details cancelled the programme as a result.

That was one of the things that worried us a little bit, because it suggested that the kind of ideology that I am talking about in my paper is still in place; that essentially that there is still a strong feeling that teaching any other language and even admitting that we teach any other language besides Hebrew could lead to a serious backlash.

Another of the things we have noted in our research and drawn attention to is the fact that people who teach Hebrew as a second language are not trained specifically to do that. There aren't any general programmes in the universities or the training colleges that concentrate on Hebrew as a Second Language as a field of study and so for some time we have been talking about the need to professionalise the teaching of HSL and train people. However, we have to be very careful about how we discuss this. If you say we are interested in the teaching of Hebrew as a *second* language, most of the people in the profession will respond that Hebrew is not a *second* language. Their feeling is that it can't be a second language. Hebrew is the language of Israel, the language of Zionism, the language of the Jews, of national identity. How could it be a second language?

And given that kind of situation, we were a little bit nervous when we initially presented our position paper to the Ministry. But we found in fact that our fears were exaggerated and that the Minister himself, the Director General, the members of the Pedagogical Secretariat, had no difficulty accepting the idea of multilingualism — at a theoretical level. They accepted our arguments that the school system has to be based on what we call three plus one: Hebrew, Arabic, English plus one other foreign language which could be any of a number of languages. First of all, as Hebrew is the national language and the language of instruction in the Jewish sector for 80% of the pupils, it must obviously be taught as a second language to the Arabic speakers. Secondly, Arabic is the language of instruction in the Arab sector and is described as a compulsory language for the seventh, eighth, ninth grades in the Jewish sector. That term compulsory is quite interesting and requires some definition; in reality only about 60% of schools offer Arabic but the word 'compulsory' is used in the policy statement. The policy statement says that in the next two years the 'compulsion' will apply to the tenth grade as well and when this has been successfully implemented, it will then be mandatory for the eleventh grade and so on.

The big problem with Arabic, although I don't want to go into the details now, is the diglossic nature of the language. It is very hard to justify teaching the vernacular in an educational setting when you have a classical variety. Students are taught Classical Arabic during the three compulsory years. But they don't get far enough in the classical language to read a newspaper and, moreover, it is not the vernacular language of the people with whom they live. There are enormous problems here.

English is the third language, and, in our context, the least contentious. When we come to the question of the fourth language there is a wide choice and much competition. There is a policy statement that immigrants are entitled to four years of instruction in their own language while they are learning Hebrew. That applies most specifically to the four and a half million Russian Jews who have arrived over the last three years from the Soviet Union. The irony here is that, having been described as Jews all their lives, when they arrive they are called Russians regardless of what part of the former Soviet Union they come from. Despite this irony, this is reasonably correct linguistically for they generally tend to speak Russian. The immigration gave us a group of people coming in at high school age who all spoke Russian, who were given instruction through Russian and who took their final school exams in Russian while learning Hebrew as well. Then, there is another group, the younger brothers and sisters of the first group, who have had their education through Hebrew and are now being instructed in Russian for Hebrew speakers. The policy does permit the teaching of immigrant languages and encourages this. Where twelve children at a school want a particular language it will be provided.

Another case of providing the language of immigrant groups is the teaching of Amharic, because we have seventy five thousand recent Ethiopian immigrants. At first there was a certain reluctance to offer this language, despite the guarantees in the policy statement. There is also provision for teaching a heritage language, for example, Yiddish and Ladino.

The fourth language may be also a language of wider diffusion, the main one being French. French has a fascinating position in the policy statement where it turns up as an alternative to compulsory Arabic! The French are pushing very hard to enshrine this choice in law and practice. The more logical place to put French would be as an alternative to English, as an international language, but the problem with that would be that nobody would learn French in preference to English. The other possible fourth languages in this category would be German, Japanese or Spanish.

The reason for giving you this outline is that my concern in the research was with the basis for language provision. I wanted to test whether the ideological argument was still essentially there. The question that the paper is concerned with 'is what is the process when there is language revitalization'. It is clear that

I am not just talking about what Fishman terms Reversing Language Shift. Language revitalization is a different case. RLS is a set of strategies for any language to try to prevent speakers giving up using it for certain functions. It can encompass policies such as those promoted by the French government to counter the encroachment of English. It can include the normativising of foreign words in the language. Reversing Language Shift is interestingly going to be a policy of the Republican Party and Senator Dole has stated that he fully supports the policy that English should be made the official language of the country. This is against a background of a feeling that the Union is threatened by multilingualism. We may have been amazed by the French feeling threatened by English, but that English feels threatened in the US is truly amazing and should allow us to understand the attempts of any language to defend itself. Joe LoBianco, director of the National Language and Literacy Institute of Australia, claims that this need to defend the language comes at a time of great insecurity. He compares the current concern with keeping the English language 'pure' with the concern to keep the Queen's head on the currency. Similarly, the American concern with maintaining English has come about at a time when the US realises that it has lost its dominance in international trade. The US has a siege mentality about this at the moment. In a recent case in a Texas court, a judge stated that a Spanish speaking mother who spoke Spanish rather than English to her child was in fact guilty of child abuse.

My concern in this paper is quite different; I am not concerned with maintaining the believed status quo or reversing language decline but rather with investigating how a community switches from one language to another and in particular how that switch occurs in the home, which is clearly the most difficult thing to achieve. One can change public language use comparatively easily. It is private language loyalty which is most firmly entrenched. A strong ideological basis is needed to cope with the great pressure involved in such a language change. I've talked elsewhere about rules for language choice and one of the strongest rules for language choice is to use a language you know. The second rule is to speak a language that the person you are speaking to knows, and the third critical rule is to use the same language with somebody that you used the last time you spoke to them.

Sue Wright (Aston University): Prompted by your paper and your introduction, I think we might discuss whether it is possible to build a model to predict the outcome — successful or not — of language maintenance, revival and revitalization. What evidence do we need to consider for a theoretical model? What are the relevant factors for revitalization? Is comparison useful — possible even? Is it valid to use Hebrew as a model or is it too singular a case? To what extent can we extrapolate from it? And, drawing on the areas of expertise of those here today, can we see these patterns replicated in the cases of Alsatian, Cornish, Ukrainian, Urdu, French and Amharic? What should we take from these various case studies?

Bernard Spolsky: It depends of course on what your model is trying to describe. For example, if it is a model dealing mainly with language acquisition, then revitalization can be defined as a special kind of language learning in which a political decision is made in order to change the linguistic repertoire of a certain group of people. If we want to change the language choices of a group, then we have to start with the knowledge of the languages that they currently have, their ability, their attitudes, their motivations. Then we have to vary the exposure to the language we wish to promote and increase the opportunities for learning. Essentially, the decision is made to change the opportunity for learning a different language. That is one way of looking at revitalization and it is a political perspective.

Another model I am interested in and one which is equally connected is the model of language choice. How do you decide in a particular situation what language to speak? There are patterns and rules: you start off in one language and having made the choice remain with that language; you opt for the one you speak best, or prefer for other reasons, in order to control the conversation; you adopt the language of the person you are talking to, particularly if you are selling something. It's a basic rule of the market place — sellers must speak the buyers' language. But once you have made the decision to use that language with that person, then you stick to that particular language; that is a sociolinguistic rule.

Helen Kelly-Holmes (Aston University): This may seem to be a micro decision but it will always have a macro dimension, a political dimension, because decisions are often made under the influence of economic necessity — this so-called economic pull which has come up so often in previous discussions in this series. The speaker of a language of an immigrant or minority community is always faced with this dilemma; if they want to sell their labour outside their community they are forced to adopt the language of the dominant group.

Bernard Spolsky: Exactly. But this instrumental economic aspect is only one of many strands which contribute to the model. We shall need to look at a wide range of factors. Of course the two models are linked; private choices depend on prior knowledge and this depends on political decisions as well as personal decisions. I think one of the interesting points we might discuss is the state of language knowledge of those instrumental in language revitalization. We assume, for example, that the people who revived Hebrew knew a lot of Hebrew. Did they? We should also say something about the kind of Hebrew they knew. Similarly, in terms of Maori, we must talk about the varieties of language people used. In both these cases — and this is a key factor for our model — we need to ask who were and are the teachers?

What sort of model do we need to account for the various factors Sue mentioned? If we knew what sort of model we were considering, then we could decide which of the facts would be relevant. The rationale for the model will determine what we will consider to be significant factors.

Sue Wright: Perhaps we could start with some remarks on overt state language planning and then move to language policy which is implicit in other official decisions and then finally come to the private domain and personal choices.

John Rex (University of Warwick): This suggests very rich fields of enquiry. I am most interested in the politics of language revitalization. The Israeli case is a somewhat particular one, and, therefore, perhaps not appropriate to use as a basis for a model. After all, Hebrew is a language that had been used for religious and scholarly purposes for many centuries by an elite group of people, which was then made the official language of a new state and vernacularised. I suggest this is not easily reproducible in any other country or place. The Maori case perhaps belongs within a different classification — one starts with a language which exists as a vernacular and which to some extent people are trying to upgrade into a more official status. We could argue that these two cases are opposite poles of revitalization. I would like to survey a number of cases along the continuum to see if there are recurrent themes.

Lewis Glinert (SOAS, London University): I have to take issue with you on the matter of elites. The language question was settled before there was a Jewish state. The school system which was set up under the British rule in the 1920s and 1930s was a conduit for pushing forward the development of a Jewish identity anchored in Israel with language as part of it. This wasn't a process imposed by an elite.

Sue Wright: I agree with John's point. The difference between the Hebrew case and the Maori one is that the revitalization of Hebrew was about looking forward. Israel was a new settlement for the Jews, a new group was coming together from different places, a new language was being introduced in a new place — albeit a language which was rooted in the religious language of the past. That is very different to the revival of Maori, which is about looking back to a tradition which is disappearing and working for the revival of a language which is under threat in its own place. Maori remains in its traditional geographical place and is waning because of past colonisation and continuing pressure from the old colonial language. These cases seem to illustrate to me a forward-looking/backward-looking dichotomy.

Muiris Ó Laoire (University College Galway): I think it would be true to say that in Ireland, language maintenance is bound up with perceptions of forward-looking/ backward-looking ideologies. There were elements in the new state who were primarily concerned with socio-economic justice and little bothered by the legacy of the past, but the Irish revivalists were committed to the maintenance of traditional values, the valuing of the linguistic heritage. The families which I have been studying, living in the East of Ireland, not in the Irish-speaking Gaeltacht, who decided for strong political reasons to adopt Irish as the language of the home were conservative in the basic sense of the term. Why these families should do this and how powerful the outside influence was in changing the language of the home is linked closely to different tendencies in the nationalist movement and is interesting from our point of view because they went against the general trend.

Charlotte Hoffmann (Salford University): I think I have to agree that Hebrew is particular. The language planning associated with Hebrew was optimistic — putting in place a language for use for future generations. Many of the instances of language revitalization that we all study are much closer to the Maori situation — the defence of a language under pressure from another language which belongs to a group which is politically and economically dominant.

Bernard Spolsky: It is not always possible to come up with universals, because the comparison can break down as situations are too different. Where there are some similarities, there are countless more differences. But I think we shall be able to make some comparisons between Irish and Hebrew. One of the aspects we can compare is age profile of the speakers when the revivals started. There were so few speakers of Maori left in the community that it was not heard by the children. Generally, when the Maori revival started, the parents no longer spoke the language, but the grandparents did. That is replicated in the Irish situation. Secondly, the other intriguing similarity for Irish, Maori and Hebrew is that there is a strong ideological basis to the language shift, a desire to break with the social situation, to go back to traditions and to create an identity. People involved in the Hebrew language revival in Israel physically moved from one country to another and isolated themselves in new communities. There is a similar tendency among the Maori to move back to homogenous communities. All groups have shown their ideological commitment in the setting up of their own schools.

Alexandra Korol (University of Manchester): Are there parallels at the level of state legislation for language policy in education?

Bernard Spolsky: We should note that Israel actually has no clearly formulated, explicit language policy, and bits of policy have emerged in various ways. Because we don't have a constitution we didn't have a stage where we sat down and stated what the official national language was to be.

In Israel the legal situation is quite complex. There is a statement on official languages in the King's Orders-in-Council in 1927 under the British Mandatory Government that said that the official languages in Palestine under the mandate were to be English, Arabic and Hebrew and the regulations stated that certain documents had to be issued in those languages. There were statements in that policy that meant judges in certain areas had to receive evidence in those languages and therefore interpreters had to be made available.

This was the only official language policy when the State of Israel came into existence in 1948 and during this period of change the state simply said (in effect) that all laws will stand until they are changed. Shortly after 1948, another regulation was issued saying the Mandatory Regulation on language remains in effect except that English is no longer one of the official languages. So that seems to leave Hebrew and Arabic as the official languages. But it's not clear to me that this document has always been interpreted in that way. There are two cases in particular which were referred to the Supreme Court and which suggest otherwise. One was a case dealing with a request in Haifa for people to have Arabic added to street signs and the other a case in Nazareth where the City Council Authorities had instructed the removal of a large sign which was only in Arabic. In both cases the court made no reference at all to that official language statement which in the past had always been quoted as the basis of language policy and thus it appeared that the policy document did not have any standing. So, in effect, language policy is reduced to practice rather than being an explicit statement.

I think these facts are important to the model. They underscore the point that policy is determined by attitudes. As soon as we focus on attitudes that determine policy, we have to ask whose attitudes count? Is it the leaders of the community and, if so, how do you become a leader of the community? Is it the administrators? Whose opinions are they taking into account? Where are the points of contact? Who is it in the family that determines which language is spoken? The anthropologists speak about a 'significant other' in the family who is important enough to make the decision. Often in this case it will be a grandparent who will keep the language alive. Once they die there would seem to be no reason to keep up that language. Whose attitude is the important one in these situations?

John Rex: In this context we might consider something I have derived from what I loosely call Barthian anthropology. It seems to me that the boundaries of an ethnic group will depend upon the project in which that group is engaged and, within the boundaries, language use will depend on this project. What very often happens is that an ethnic minority which is at a disadvantage, as in a situation of class conflict, may be mobilising to fight that situation, and, inter alia, they may say that they want the strength that comes from sharing the language even though they may be putting themselves in an inferior position economically by not speaking the official language. That would seem to encapsulate the Maori position. The Zionist project was a unique project in that the Barthian boundaries were supplemented by actual, new, territorial boundaries in a new place. Despite the rather negative attitude towards Zionism amongst Yiddish speakers which you mention in your paper — and other tensions that we know about — there was a general consensus amongst the Jewish population on what their boundaries were — and, of course, they were not primarily linguistic but religious. I think in this context language is perhaps less important for symbolic purposes than it might be in others.

Sue Wright: But of course very important in the long term for building a community of communication from disparate elements, in a society of immigrants from different linguistic backgrounds.

Bernard Spolsky: Although bear in mind that Yiddish would have also fulfilled that function.

Sue Wright: Do you think that the Semitic base of Hebrew might also have had an attraction?

Lewis Glinert: The attempt to revitalize Hebrew was less of a challenge to the Sephardic population because they were actually Arabic speakers and it was far easier for the children from this group to switch to a Semitic language than it was for the children of Yiddish speakers.

Frank Knowles (Aston University): I was wondering how far the candidacy of Hebrew was compromised by the scruples which many Orthodox believers had that using Hebrew for secular purposes was a profanity.

Bernard Spolsky: The ultra-orthodox Jews rejected the movement completely and they would not accept Hebrew until 1970. They speak Hebrew today in public, but they do not use it at home. During the period of revitalization, the orthodox Jewish person living in Palestine rejected Hebrew secularism, with few exceptions. Perhaps I can draw together some points here. We're looking at a group whose members made individual decisions about language use and whose linguistic choices and attitudes brought about the linguistic policies that we have today.

The role of home language is key, I think, and the decisions made at family level were crucial, particularly between 1905 and 1912/13, when the critical decisions were made to speak Hebrew at home. Those decisions were being made in Europe as well as in Israel. For example, a Jew growing up in Odessa in 1907 had various choices of politics, language, identity. If he decided to remain Orthodox, he continued to speak Yiddish at home, and to study Hebrew and to learn the co-territorial vernacular for dealing with non-Jews. On the other hand, he could opt to become a believer in the socialist future of the world etc. and set out to learn Russian. Or he could have decided to become a scientist or academic and learn German and French and go to Switzerland. Or he could have become a Jewish nationalist and this would present him with two distinct choices: if he opted for the secular, cultural, non-territorial choice then his language would be Yiddish, the language of the workers. Out of that came the Yiddish secular movement which was very strong in Europe and America. In America there were Yiddish secular day schools. Or he could choose Zionism, which had elements of socialism, the idea of returning to a land, Israel — though not necessarily — and the idea of Hebrew being re-established as a secular language. As several of you have said, the revitalization was not a return to something that existed, it was a use of tradition to build something for the future. The part I am interested in here is the initial stage — the switch in the home.

If we open it up beyond that — then the model will have to deal with everything, including French government protection of the French language and the English Only Movement in America as being a defence of the language. I would like to get a model that concentrates on the forces from outside that account for the switches in the family.

Julian Edge (Aston University): If one is trying to model across these contexts, far and away the most impressive approach I have come across is your own preference model. It is exactly in those terms one can start to pull together the various observations of conditions under which language choice has been seen to happen, either typically or in a graded way. I think you are absolutely right to unpick the conditions and have very simple dichotomous choices and then pull it together into an interactive model. And you have to start — as you do — with social context.

John Rex: This may be apparent to all but I feel it still needs to be stated. In most societies you have to distinguish between the public domain — that of the culture, the market, the welfare state, what happens in the official language — and, on the other hand, the private area in such a society, where there may be a recognition of the right of people to practice their religion, their language, their customs in the private sphere. When one looks at the Maori case and others, the social context is clearly multilayered. These groups have two social contexts: their relationship with what we might term the mainstream, the dominating society and the dynamic within their own discrete group. How far is the desire to have a language sustained simply part of the desire to sustain their separate communities, part of the defences that they must use? Is it something more? Is it to press the state towards bilingualism? Within that framework somehow or other one could construct a matrix and put a whole number of different cases into different boxes.

Bernard Spolsky: Perhaps we don't see enough of the context as linguists or recognise enough cases where language has been temporarily used for such purposes.

Sue Wright: But that is precisely what is interesting — the impact of the greater context on the individual decision. It is very difficult to look at this question in isolation; we must always look at the context.

Bernard Spolsky: Which parts of the context?

Manjula Datta (University of North London): It depends on the situation which people find themselves in. In the work I have been doing in Asian language communities in London, language choice in the family appears to depend on so many different factors, feeding into the choices bilingual generations make, and some of them will be political and economic choices, or choices at the level of personal relationships. It is so complex that I am not sure we can build a model apart from where you have this list of preferences.

Bernard Spolsky: The perfect model accounts for binary choices. The preference model states that you do not have to have all the conditions and no one condition is ever enough. Lots of different cases will lead to the same kind of choice being made. It is not merely instrumental versus ideological. For example, once Hebrew was established as the language of the community because of ideologically motivated choices, the instrumental reasons, the need to learn it to benefit from being part of the community, came into play. The model has to include all the factors, but not all of them will be relevant in all situations.

Lewis Glinert: If we are going to look at a language choice model, then it is vital to build into it the question of motivation which every teacher builds into their model of success in language learning.

Andrea Young (Université de Mulhouse): I believe motivation is fundamental to the preference model and perhaps I can try to define it. The concepts involved in motivation: goals, needs, attitudes, desire, choice — these general concepts reappear but there are always differences which are obvious from the context and this could be key in the model. In the Maori context we are talking about children in the home being the initiators of language change — in fact we are looking at three contexts: the individual context of the child and all the different variables; the immediate environment of the family/parental attitudes, the status of the language in the family, the encouragement given to the child; finally the sociolinguistic cultural environment and all the influences that can be brought to bear on the individual — status of the language in society, and economic-related status, religious status, educational policies. In the Hebrew context it is not just the education system plus the children but a whole society decision. Motivation is different in these different contexts, affected by different influences and perhaps this is one key to the conceptual model we are searching for.

Bernard Spolsky: On the basis of what we know about language revitalization and how potential speakers make decisions when presented with choices we could ask whether we can predict what will happen to Maori. What will be the critical evidence that we as experts want to see before we will be able to say that this case is successful? What is success? Is it family language use, or the establishment of Maori identity? What I have been looking for in the Maori case are children speaking Maori outside of the classroom.

Sue Wright: That would be a good example of language choice that is not motivated by what we have been terming contextual pressures. That might be seen as choice which indicates allegiance or simple ease in the language.

Bernard Spolsky: It is quite a long way down the road to revitalization. In the case of Hebrew this was quite a late development.

Lewis Glinert: I think this leads on to a tantalising part of the problem which concerns what happened after the British took over in Israel. I would like to mention a statistic. In 1917, when the British took over and there were 65,000 Jews in The Holy Land, the native speakers of Hebrew were by no means in the majority. Thirty year later there were 650,000 Hebrew speakers, so there was an influx of nearly ten times this number, nearly all of them Yiddish speakers, and yet they all could speak Hebrew. To me, the tantalising question is, what happened along the way? How much does it have to do with people growing up and having to decide when they were adults about their language? To what extent did economic, political and ideological factors motivate them to be Hebrew speakers.

Alexandra Korol: We have to consider too the global influences at the time — the Second World War, the Holocaust, the population of survivors coming back homeless, finding their 'home' in Israel, making language choices that were loyalty choices.

Bernard Spolsky: But in 1910 this was not relevant. After the pogroms of 1882, there was the beginning of a massive emigration from Eastern Europe. Huge numbers of Jews left and most of them went west. A tiny number of them went to Palestine and of that small group some went on to America during World War One and did not return. These people came to Israel out of choice and their motivation was different to that of later immigrants. Once Hebrew was established in 1923–24, it was the public language of the Jewish population in Palestine. Anybody arriving there was under the normal pressure of any immigrant to learn the language of the new country, and was coming because they had nowhere else to go. Now they were coming into an established situation where Hebrew was the language of the Jewish community. There was, therefore, a strong instrumental motivation. But the revitalization had taken place earlier. The events of the Second World War were very significant, but they do not account for the language switch that took place in many homes, nor do they help us understand how Hebrew became established within the community by 1920.

Muiris Ó Laoire: The study of the revitalization of Hebrew was for me key in trying to explain why some families in Ireland made a switch in the home. I came up against what Nahir called 'the great leap' in the revitalization of Hebrew. This is the inexplicable stage where children learn the language, and actually start to speak it outside the classroom. For me this is the fascinating aspect of revitalization and I have yet to witness it in the revitalization of Gaelic in Ireland. I would like to know why, how and when this happens.

Bernard Spolsky: The children have to see it as an identity they want. There has to be 'youth culture' appeal.

Frank Knowles: And speakers must also lose — or never have — the self consciousness which many people feel when speaking a foreign language.

Stephen Barbour (Middlesex University): In other situations this does seem to be a significant factor in revitalization. For example, there seems at present to be a growing attraction amongst young people for Welsh-medium culture.

Charlotte Hoffmann: Yes, and it has been noted that there is a gender bias, with girls more likely to promote the use of the language.

Bernard Spolsky: What we need to discover is how young people become convinced of this attractiveness; how this separate culture of their own evolves; and how you can sell a particular language to this culture if you want to maintain or revitalize it.

Frank Knowles: I think also the role of the teaching medium should not be underestimated. A hundred years ago it was English in the classroom and Welsh in the playground and today it is the other way round.

Stephen Barbour: And language is by no means the only criterion: Welsh-medium schools are very attractive to many parents for reasons which may have little to do with wanting their children to speak Welsh or have a Welsh identity. In Eastern Wales, many individuals, who are monoglot English speakers themselves, choose to send their children to Welsh medium schools because they perceive the education to be better and they note that these schools often have better results.

Sharon Imtiaz (University of Warwick): This brings to mind field work I carried out in Pakistan and the attempts of the Pakistan Language Board to implement Kashmiri as the language of education. A great deal of faith was placed in hoped for effects of childhood school education. The Kashmiris were overly optimistic about what could be achieved in terms of language revitalization by school education. And this is particularly problematic in a situation with many competing languages. Very soon the Kashmiri child will in theory be learning — in what can be a difficult physical environment with poor resources — English from kindergarten to college, Urdu from primary to secondary with the option of dropping Urdu for English, if Sciences are taken, and then three years of compulsory Kashmiri. For 90% of pupils this is not compatible with the languages spoken in the home. This is a considerable burden on the family but there are great ideological reasons behind it.

My point is that policy makers place an enormous amount of faith on the power of school language, and I, myself, am quite sceptical about the trickle-down effect that is hoped for.

Tom Bloor (Aston University): I could perhaps mention some of the problems that arise from the language policies of the education system in Ethiopia. The government is currently promoting a form of equal recognition among the languages, but it is inconceivable that there can be anything resembling complete egalitarianism for all languages since current figures suggest that there are approximately 90 languages. Most are spoken by small minority groups. Nine linguistic areas have been set up and the organisation is on the territorial principle — so it is too bad if you are in the wrong one linguistically. Nine vernaculars constitute the languages of education in Ethiopia and still many are educated through a second language. The situation is very complicated and not very feasible, although it is dominated by commendable sentimental considerations. Here, too, tremendous faith is put in the school system at the expense of the instrumental considerations — contrary to what one would expect, since in practice it is the instrumental which usually wins. One of the most surprising things is that one of the languages of the nine regions is Arabic. However, despite its standing in other parts of the world, it is seen very much as a fringe language and usually a language of immigrants.

Sue Wright: And has this official regard for language difference within the education system been of help in language maintenance? What is really interesting here is the way that either government or power elites may make language policy without regard for the choices made at family level and if you omit any of the levels then the model will be faulty in predicting long-term language behaviour. After all regard for language difference in the education system was also a feature of former Yugoslavia, which makes, I think, a graphic illustration of the uselessness of supporting linguistic diversity without anchoring it into wider socio-economic and political considerations and without addressing the tensions between linguistic groups resulting from conflicts in these areas.

Tom Bloor: The status of Amharic in Ethiopia is high, influenced both by education and religion. And there are — of course — tensions between groups. My point is that I expected instrumental considerations to have more of an effect than they do here. On a practical, economic level, it is easier to operate a state where there is only one language. I am not saying that this is the way to deal with the situation, but it would be cheaper to run a state where only one language is spoken. There are all sorts of problems that arise from multilingualism — Ethiopia is a prime example of an education system where a small budget is dealing with too many languages and not enough teachers or materials for most of them.

Bernard Spolsky: But you could have a monolingual education system that accepts multilingualism. Traditional Jewish education was always conducted in Yiddish in Eastern Europe but the subject of study was always Hebrew. It was accepted that you teach in the language of the home, but you acquired the standard version. To a certain extent that must be what happens in Norway. The two official languages are taught in school but everyone continues to speak the local dialect. There has been much debate as to which of the two varieties should be taught but less emphasis on learning the standard language and giving up dialectal difference.

Charlotte Hoffmann: You seem to be saying that modern language policies are embracing multilingualism and even promoting it. Are you?

Bernard Spolsky: People are upset about language loss and the people who are making the decisions in the home — which are the critical ones — are going in the wrong direction according to those of us who believe in multilingualism. The pressure is in the direction of monolingualism because it is easier for the education system. But from my work with the Navajo, it is clear that bilingualism is positive. They have developed their own reading materials and have spread the idea that children who learn to read in their own language first will have a better grasp of a second language later. In traditional East European Jewish schools, Yiddish-speaking children came to school and were taught to read Herbrew, the language of the religious texts, from the very beginning. So, what we need is tolerance of bi- and multilingualism, even if there is a monolingual school system.

The problem is this force for uniformity. There is strong pressure towards uniformity, first of all for selecting the same language and secondly for selecting one variety of that language. Once you put a language into a school system you start promoting a normative form and who controls the prescriptive process — *the normativisation* — becomes an interesting question. I like the theory that people try and control language through choice of variety. However, this does not quite work with Hebrew interestingly enough. The Hebrew normativists were individualists, never met and never agreed on norms. What you do have in Hebrew is the belief that there is a norm, and every native speaker knows that he or she does not follow the norm and does make mistakes.

Fortunately, counteracting the pressure for uniformity, there is also very strong pressure going the other way as well — towards diversity. For some interesting reason, middle class intellectuals favour diversity, and language revitalization tends to come out of this intellectual middle class which believes in the value of diversity — perhaps because its members can afford it. Take, for example, the situation in Ethiopia with the different elements trying to build a state. Is it that they cannot afford to let all these languages go or is it simply politics? Is it simply that they want to break the power of the Amharic speakers by encouraging all these other languages, just as in Kashmir you spend the extra to establish Kashmir as a language because you need another symbol?

Tom Bloor: Yes, it is a lot of those things, but I would argue that it is not just a universal truth for all time that intellectual middle class people promote and value multilingualism or that multilingualism is always used positively. For example, in South Africa, a policy of multilingualism was used by the apartheid government to keep people from unifying and forming a state with a different government. It is not simply the case that multilingualism is good or that middle class intellectuals favour it.

Charlotte Hoffmannn: I don't think we are considering the pressure of alternatives. In the Maori situation, in the UK situation, in a number of the situations we are studying, people have the alternative of using English and this is always an attractive proposition. To what extent was there a realistic alternative to Hebrew in the 1920s?

Bernard Spolsky: In the period I am referring to, most Jews in Palestine spoke Yiddish.

Charlotte Hoffmann: But could they see, at the time, that it was going to be a viable language of a future state?

Bernard Spolsky: I believe they were thinking of their own existence. However German may also have been an alternative. Arabic as I mentioned was not, since Palestine was under Turkish rule and the growth of Arab nationalism at this time was in opposition to Turkish rule and so not really a viable option. French was quite a strong choice in some areas as long as Rothschild was supporting education in the villages. But once this stopped in 1899 then French was no longer an option. German became particularly important from 1895 on when there was a strong language diffusion policy as part of the unification of Germany. The consuls and missionaries worked together to establish German in the schools and it was becoming a language of education in Palestine between 1895 and 1914. After the First World War, Germans were no longer present and the British occupied the area. However, none of these options was as strong as English was and is in the Maori case or the Irish case.

Julian Edge: In terms of factors in a model, I'd like to refer back to the language of the paper, where Professor Spolsky was describing the decisions of that time. What struck me were expressions such as 'the drive for assertion of superiority', the 'bitter struggle', 'physical violence', the 'persecution' of Yiddish, the drive for 'purity and cleanliness', the drive to establish a 'pioneering', 'masculine' 'language'. I wonder if one can't also see what was to come, foreshadowed in those words and in that movement and in some sense one could say that what was happening then on the very small scale has happened again on the large scale. I wonder if it is really enough to describe this simply as a strong ideology and therefore motivation for language change. Wasn't winning a country, a territory, a significant point also? And to do that the nationalists marshalled language as they did other organising principles which would help their goal. They were ultimately successful in demonstrating their own superiority, successful in fulfilling in their own terms this view of what was to be. So winning is as motivational to people as whatever ideology they express — and its relationship to adoption of a certain language so banal that we don't even mention it. For me, the great difference between Hebrew and Maori is that Hebrew speakers won — they are the dominant group; Maori speakers didn't — they are not. The two situations are so fundamentally different that comparisons are going to be strained.

Bernard Spolsky: There is perhaps a general one, which is that the language of instruction in Israeli state schools in the Jewish sector and that includes several different types of schools — that language is Hebrew — and education in the state schools in the Arab sector is in Arabic. Secondly, there is provision for the compulsory teaching of Arabic in Jewish schools and the compulsory teaching of Hebrew in the Arab schools and a general requirement and a general acceptance of the fact that English is taught throughout both school systems. We could contrast that with New Zealand where the *Kohango reo* movement is still very limited.

In another way you are right; comparisons are not always useful. As a language, Maori is also very idealistic; one of the problems that faces the Maori is that there are so many tribes and they speak different tribal dialects and the answer seems to be to revive the tribal dialect because Maori is a collective 'colonial' term, whereas the identity lies in the tribe. At the same time they are building a very postmodern Maori identity.

Lewis Glinert: This idea of the strategy of the 'repulsive' attitude towards Yiddish and its role in the revitalization of Hebrew interests me. This is in stark contrast to the very positive attitude towards English amongst many of the communities whose languages are threatened by encroaching English. The Asian community in Britain is an example. I'm suggesting, perhaps not totally seriously, that if we could make the English language repulsive to the younger members of these communities, this would give the survival of the Asian community languages a chance.

Manjula Datta: This is the great dilemma, because those of us who are working in this area do not want to see minority linguistic groups ghettoised by not participating in the mainstream language and all that goes with it. We need to ensure that young people, who are able, have access to what in Britain is still a resolutely monolingual higher education system for example. At the same time we need to make English less magnetic — so that there is room for language maintenance. And I don't mean that one language pushes out another. I do believe firmly that bilingualism is an asset and language enhancing rather than problematic. I mean make room in people's motivation — give them a desire for real competence in two languages.

Julian Edge: Perhaps it's not even a matter of levity to say 'well if you can get people to feel a repugnance for English then that will be a good motivational trick to pull'. Because one can observe that tendency and perhaps the extent to which the dominant language evokes repugnance in those people who are under linguistic pressure will be of use to those who seek to revitalize or maintain a minority language. But I suggest that if it is effective, there will be unwanted side effects. For example, how can we control 'repulsion': thus far and no further, enough for language maintenance, not far enough for societal schism?

Helen Kelly-Holmes: And we mustn't forget the individual desires of the child. While I recognise the legitimate wish to hand down the language and the culture of the group, there is a real danger of over-zealous parents imposing an identity upon children that is not necessarily their experience. By suggesting, for example, to young people living in Britain that English is unattractive as a language is ridiculous because it is a part of their identity and it is also important to recognise that this identity and experience is different from that of their parents and grandparents. These groups who are anxious to keep their language alive must respect the British part of these children's identity and strive for a compromise. This imposition of an identity was, perhaps, the reason why the revival of Irish was so unsuccessful. Through the teaching of Irish, young people felt the imposition of an identity to which they could not relate and which did not value or relate to their own experience or reality.

Manjula Datta: I do recognise what you say about part of the children's identity being British but I would like to believe what Jim Cummins says about bilingual children having a dual identity. In the cases we see, both in our research and in the business of teaching practice, it does seem to me that language loss is also about loss of identity. In the British context, Asian parents have to create a strength of identity for their children which will be able to withstand the racism they will meet.

Helen Kelly-Holmes: That's very defensive. If young people, their communities and the agencies of the government, such as the education service, recognise that dual identity is possible and that the two inheritances are not mutually exclusive then this seems a healthier alternative to me than the enforced preservation of language and culture not fully recognising that the younger generation is evolving into new forms of both legacies.

Li Wei (University of Newcastle upon Tyne): Exactly. People who combine two identities, have a distinct identity and in order to have this distinct identity they have to keep something and lose something. They may have to lose their mother tongue but they may keep their way of eating, respect for elders, their dress code. That would still give them a distinct identity. There are other ways to show that they are a distinct group. It would seem to me that it is quite impossible for 'authorities' or the older generation to manipulate this identity. It arises on an interface that is too complex to fully appreciate as it is happening let alone control.

Bernard Spolsky: Well, people try. The Samoans in New Zealand are working hard at language maintenance through three distinct strategies: one is the church which has become a context for maintaining language and culture. Religion can be very important in preserving a language. Then there are friendship groups: parents have various rules — not playing with non-Samoans at the weekend, for example. Then the parents try to send the children back to Samoa regularly. This is active maintenance.

Sue Wright: You can find such grass roots 'policy' decisions in the various linguistic minority groups in the UK. The community is kept together by the mosque or the gurdwara, marriage within the group is encouraged, the ease of travel makes frequent trips to the country of origin possible. But all of this may work for language maintenance or against it. For example, in very traditional, patriarchal groups, the girls who wish to break away from the constraints they may experience will reject the language along with the arranged marriage, the extended visits to elderly relatives, as all part of a set of actions designed to compel them to observe certain norms that they wish to reject. In other contexts and for other younger members of the group, religion, friendship networks, trips to a country where the language is widely spoken may be a great motivation to keep the language as part of one's repertoire.

Mike Grover (Multilingual Matters): Is there not perhaps a continuum of identities and, for those in a bilingual situation, a continuum of languages? We seem to be drifting into assuming that second generation British must either reject their ancestral heritage wholesale or keep it wholesale. We ought to keep in mind the reality: as a bilingual, you are sitting somewhere between the two languages and the two identities. Then you can negotiate your own particular identity and even your own particular language.

Sharon Imtiaz: I think this is in fact happening in Britain, especially with emerging identities; many Asian youths are speaking among themselves in a language which is neither Panjabi, Urdu or English. It is their own language and no less a distinct language for not being codified. In London there has emerged a very distinct London Jamaican patois. I find that children at a very young age are very adept at choosing which they consider to be the appropriate variety depending on the context and the person to whom they are speaking.

Bencie Woll (City University): In the societies of which we have experience, there are few homogenous groups. We should think about the implications of this. Effectively we shall be 'reviving' a language for speakers for whom it is not a heritage language, teaching it to non-members as well as members of the community. This happens with Welsh and to a lesser extent Gaelic. It is a difficulty for community language provision. Often a standardised language is offered to speakers of non-standardised dialects or a national language to speakers of regional languages.

Ken George (University of Plymouth): Numbers are fundamental. You can't have too much splitting. There is a certain critical mass. As soon as you have that size of group, that number of speakers, then maintenance or revival becomes feasible. You need to persuade people into the speech community. That is why the Hebrew case study is fascinating. People were persuaded in.

Mike Grover: I'm thinking of personal experience here. Is it not true that this persuasion and so the successful maintenance of a minority language can often be traced back to the evangelism and commitment of perhaps one person who establishes a group? In terms of the Finnish community in England, Hannele Branch started a movement that began twenty years ago and which has spread right across the country and undoubtedly without her energy, the Finnish community would not have the Sunday schools which have kept some competence in the language amongst the younger members.

On a different point, is there any evidence that different positions in the family will have an effect on who acquires the language and to what degree of competence?

Manjula Datta: Yes, we've been doing work on this — both position in family and gender. I have a feeling from the data that is emerging that first children keep the language better. But other influences are very important, for example the role of grandparents in child care is a factor.

On another point, we seem to be making the assumption that everyone acts sensibly and with sensitivity. This isn't the case at all, of course. Language is a very emotive affair. In a recent case that I was studying, the second child, who was a male, refused to speak the home language and would not respond, even though he was punished for speaking English in the home. I can't imagine that this set of experiences will have a positive outcome in language maintenance. I think this proves how important personal attitude and motivation are, along with community and family initiatives.

Bencie Woll: One often sees that only one child in a family is truly bilingual and quite often it is the eldest child but this is by no means a set rule. The factors influencing why that child is fluent are numerous but I agree that family relationships are influential.

Bernard Spolsky: The normal pattern in an immigrant family is that the eldest child goes to school and brings home the new language and by the time the younger siblings are at school age you will find that the household has switched to the new language.

Manjula Datta: We are finding that although we have many parents who are ideologically motivated to maintain the family language, the intrusion of the English language into the families through a variety of media is detrimental to bilingualism. The various populations of Asian origin have lived in Britain for over thirty years and the languages are just surviving, but there is no way that bilingualism is properly valued by society at large. At the moment, the Asian community is in a state of panic with regard to the transmission of language skills. However there is some revitalization going on, with, for example, cable TV broadcasting Indian programmes. However, without a language policy there is little hope and the National Curriculum wants only standard English and bilingual children are not taken into account. I want people to think about this.

Sue Wright: Playing devil's advocate here, I want to ask, why should we keep these languages?

Manjula Datta: For our own identity; we need to save them in order to survive. No matter how well a person is doing, if they don't have an identity this has a detrimental effect on the welfare of the person.

John Rex: But, why should we bother if languages die out? It seems a very unsatisfactory answer to simply say that there are X thousand languages in the world and we don't want this number to drop. Some say, as Manjula does, that it is about identity and the loss of identity connected to language loss. I'm not absolutely sure this is true because people could still have a very strong and separate identity without a separate language.

Stephen Barbour: I agree. I don't think that the anglophone Irish have much problem with identity. The nationalists made an issue of this but it never really got off the ground. They have not lost their sense of ethnicity even though they do not speak Gaelic and, in the case of Irish Americans, there is a very strong sense of ethnic identity even though the language was lost many generations ago.

Sue Wright: To change tack and argue on the other side, what about if you agree with a very weak form of the Sapir-Whorf hypothesis which says that your language and world view go together? Will language loss and language shift affect your way of apprehending the world? If humanity loses a language does it lose something valuable in terms of biodiversity?

Tom Bloor: The Sapir-Whorf argument is that ideas expressed through the language that is lost are also lost, but I do not think this is true.

Sue Wright: No, I'm not claiming that the idea will be lost. It is always possible to translate and to invent terms where necessary to cope with concepts new to a language and culture. But, as linguists, we all know that if you come across a concept in another language, it is difficult to comprehend it at first and that our ways of portraying it and rendering it into the target language make for subtle transformations of the original idea. We mediate it through *our* own experience. Even in related languages, an elegant line of argument that is easy in one language can be very difficult to express as persuasively in another. So when a language goes, the concept *in its original form* goes.

Frank Knowles: I agree that the loss of a language means the disappearance of a way of looking at things, a particular way of relating to the world and describing that in words, and such a disappearance reduces human diversity. The way we react to the world is conditioned by all sorts of things and is expressed through language in ways that are quite idiosyncratic for many people. When there is a disappearance, certain things become ineffable, and therefore an insight into human existence has been lost.

Sharon Imtiaz: I can see this as language change but I can't see that there is a total loss. For me the bigger problem is that there is, of course, the human rights issue — the right of a person to express him or herself in a language. But I don't think we can go on preserving languages for the sake of it, a museum of language as linguists are prone to want to do, because language preservation may itself be a violation of rights where speakers are actually exercising their rights to opt for language shift.

Manjula Datta: You say it is a human right, I think it is life itself. When language has gone, the generation following after will have less of that culture and subsequent generations will have nothing, because language is absolutely, inextricably linked with culture. For example, the achievement of Asian children in school is largely the result of the family infrastructure — which in turn comes from religion, language and other carriers of those cultural values.

John Rex: But, what about the case of young male Sikhs in England who have not retained their Panjabi but who are still deeply involved in the affairs of the Punjab and for whom there is no question of any identity but Sikh Panjabi?

Sue Wright: But their involvement with issues in the Punjab — which will of course take place in Panjabi — will be subtly different from someone who can assess all the information in the original and pick up the inferences and sub-texts that are present in that original.

Bernard Spolsky: Another example to add to John's is the Jewish community in Alexandria at the time of Phylo, some two thousand years ago. The community did not speak much Hebrew, but maintained its identity after it switched to Greek. To a certain extent some of the Jewish community that switched to German or French did manage to maintain some very interesting identities and the North American Jewish Community preserve a very strong Jewish identity to an certain extent. But, I agree that it does not seem to last more than a generation or two.

John Rex: But if you have a mosque where Muslim youths are taught in English, I don't think they are very readily going to lose their Muslim identity.

Bernard Spolsky: I suspect that they will have trouble in the long term. Identities may remain strong for a generation or two then after that it is not clear.

Ken George: We were faced with this problem in Cornwall, Cornish died out as a community language in 1800 and in the 1980s we were twice faced with the question of whether Cornwall should be a Euro-constituency. Cornwall is not part of England yet it is treated as if it were. Arguments were put forward that Cornwall should be treated as a special case on the basis of its regional, historical and cultural identity. One part of that cultural identity was deemed to be the language, even though that language had died out two hundred years before. It suddenly assumed immense symbolic significance. This is an example of people's perception of a separate community existing, even after the widespread use of the language has died out.

Bernard Spolsky: I think our question has been answered — you can have an identity without a language but you will automatically invent a language to fit that identity! A lot of national languages were in fact invented for that very purpose. In terms of the preference model, language is not a necessary condition but it is such a highly desirable condition that if there is no common language, one will be invented — as Bahasa was in Indonesia.

Stephen Barbour: I don't think we're any closer to a model, although the elements that must impact on it have been well-aired. I'd just like us to return to the macro level for a moment and recognise the role of the state. In Europe monolingualism seems to me to be very much bound up with the development of the modern type of nation state where there is often the drive for the total control of the central authority in all areas. Perhaps this is the key reason why minority languages are threatened. Our societal conditioning gives us a strong ideology of monolingualism and therefore bi- or multilingualism is seen as a problem — which, from a sensible linguistic point of view, it is not. But it's very hard to break through this viewpoint. I do not want to give any simplistic explanation for this, but surely it has something to do with control. For example, the insistence on an exclusive cultivation of standard English at school is about social control — partly the state exercising control, but dressed up as empowerment. Preserving other languages is seen as necessarily causing marginalisation and as something negative. On the other hand, while I do accept that there is a need to protect these languages, there is also a very powerful economic need to learn English. Therefore, I think it is useful to separate the economic from the ideological and to always be aware that if we want to protect language diversity we have to fundamentally change the attitude of the majority to bi- or multilingualism.

Bernard Spolsky: In the case of Hebrew, the intriguing thing is that those that pushed this ideology of monolingualism were all themselves multilingual. But still they insisted that the school system and their children become monolingual. They did not believe in monolingualism for its own sake but they believed in the need for Hebrew monolingualism. Where does this idea of monolingualism come from? Your analysis may have elements of truth.

An Historical Perspective on the Revival of Irish Outside the Gaeltacht, 1880–1930, with Reference to the Revitalization of Hebrew

Muiris Ó Laoire
Irish Language Department, University College Galway, Ireland

Revival and Revitalization

One invariably finds the position of Irish mentioned in any discussion of language revival or revitalization. In the past, it has been posited as an example of language revivalist efforts gone wrong, but recent reappraisals would emphasise a more successful story.

The historical restoration of Irish, which was initiated at the end of the last century, and which continues to the present day, is an example of language revival, as distinct from language revitalization. It would be true to say that Irish revitalization has not occurred to any great extent since 1922, but, on the other hand, it must be acknowledged that Irish revivalist efforts during the same periods have resulted in an appreciable increase in the number of people who have acquired some knowledge of the language (Dorian, 1987).

Development and expansion of the language could be described in terms of secondary bilingualism and is attributable in most cases to the promotion of the language in and through the educational system. Irish, or *An Ghaeilge* is a compulsory subject in all primary and post-primary schools and the average Irish person is exposed to 13 years instruction in the language. The production of secondary bilinguals through the educational system compensates somewhat for the demise in numbers of native speakers in the *Gaeltacht* or all-Irish communities, which are mainly situated mainly along the western sea-board.

The present paper purports to ascertain why revivalist efforts, which began at the end of the last century, and which have been endorsed and subsumed by native government since 1922, have not led to a revitalization of the type associated with Hebrew (Spolsky, 1991). It analyses in particular the historical issues which surrounded revivalist efforts outside the *Gaeltacht* community, with a view to understanding the conditions and processes which should have existed for revitalization.

Inability to observe these processes at first hand and dependence on scant contemporary descriptions render this understanding all the more difficult. However, it is hoped that a revision of the early stages of the historical process which underlay the revival of Irish may have salutary significance for contemporary language planning in Ireland and elsewhere.

We do not, as of yet, have a good history of language planning in Ireland, in that much which has been written about the Irish language and its revival is flawed by a tendency to draw certain assumptions about the importance of the language, which clouds the possibility of any dispassionate analysis. It is also hoped that the approach adopted in this paper may, therefore, begin to fill this gap and pave the way for a more objective analytic discourse.

The Revitalization of Hebrew

Cross references will be made to the revitalization of Hebrew for two reasons. Firstly, it provides a model against which the Irish case can be tested, although one must avoid any simplified and decontextualised analogy. Analogous references to the revival of Hebrew have, in fact, always been a feature of the dialogue on the revival of Irish. It is interesting to note that the editorial of the Irish language newspaper, *Fáinne An Lae* (Daybreak) as early as 1924, considered the revitalization of Hebrew as a paradigm for the revival of Irish, with the subtle implication that efforts towards achieving revitalization in Ireland, could at best imitate the linguistic transformation which occurred in Palestine.

Until recent times, dispassionate, theoretical analysis has by and large been absent from debate on the language, so, a parallel study is relevant to the study of language planning in Ireland, in that it brings the dimension of external comparative critique to the discipline. This consequently safeguards against a discussion that may be flawed by an over-introspective paralysis of analysis, which, unfortunately has been a feature of past studies in this area.

Gaeltacht and *Galltacht*

The term revival can only realistically be used in the context of the Galltacht (the speech community existing *outside* the *Gaeltacht*), because here, by the end of the nineteenth century, the language had passed out of all use and was devoid of any specific function. The present study will concentrate entirely, therefore, on the area defined traditionally as the *Galltacht*.

While both issues of language revival and language maintenance tend to be encompassed within the scope of general analysis on the Irish language Revival, it may be helpful for present purposes to isolate the *Gaeltacht* and *Galltacht* realities one from the other, in order to achieve a better understanding of certain features of language revival, which explain why a language revitalization did not take place. In one sense, the Irish language in the *Gaeltacht* constituted a significant support system for revivalist efforts elsewhere, and while the dual reality was espoused and subsumed into governmental concentration and planning since 1922; rarely, in practice, did language maintenance and language revival policies cross paths or cross-fertilise.

The Background to Language Revival: A Lack of Clarity

It appears that there was a lack of clarity about what exactly constituted language restoration in the new state. The rather amorphous concept of a linguistic restoration was inherited from a certain confusion among the Gaelic League propagandists themselves regarding the exact nature of the *athbheochan* or language revival. Whatever aspirations the founders of the Gaelic League may have had, they did not, formulate any working definition of what they meant by a revival. They certainly did not write anything definite into their constitution about having Irish spoken by *all* the people of Ireland, nor was there any declared intention or objective about the total replacement of English by Irish (Ó Cuiv, 1969: 128).

Hyde, for example who posited the continuation of the Irish tradition as an ideological base for the restoration of the language, vacillated in his under-standing of what constituted a language revival. Daly (1974) has described an early article of his, entitled *A Plea for the Irish Language* published in *The Dublin University Review* in 1886, as an article of major significance in the study of Hyde's political and cultural development in that, for the first time, he formulated ideas which were to become fundamental principles of the Gaelic League propaganda in the years to come. In this article, Hyde did not envisage a revival occurring outside the *Gaeltacht*. It is interesting to note what he proposed. He advocated a social and economical restoration of the *Gaeltacht* rather than the revival of the language in the country as a whole.

He wrote:

> There is no use arguing the advantage of making Irish the language of our newspapers and clubs because. This is and ever shall be an impossibility. But for several reasons we wish to arrest the language of its downward path and if we cannot spread it (and I do not believe we very much can) we will at least prevent it from dying out, and make sure that those who speak it now will also transmit it unmodified to their descendants.

Had Hyde persisted in this policy, which was apparently aimed at language maintenance in the *Gaeltacht*, the Gaelic League would have persisted perhaps in quite a different course of action from that which it historically pursued — the aim being the social and economic development of the *Gaeltacht* areas rather than the restoration of the language throughout the country as a whole.

In a later speech given to the *Cumann Gaelach* (The Irish Society) in America published in *The Irish American* 27 June, 1891, he referred again to what he meant by language revival :

> I do not for a moment advocate making Irish the language of the country at large or of the National Parliament ... What I want to see is Irish established as a living language for all time among the million or half-million who still speak it along the west coast, and to ensure that the language will hold a favourable place in teaching institutions and govern-ment examinations.

It is clear, therefore, that Hyde never envisaged the Irish language actually supplanting English as the dominant language of the country. Even in his celebrated *Necessity for the de-Anglicisation of Ireland* oration in 1893, which marked the beginning of *Conradh na Gaeilge* (the movement for the restoration of Irish), he re-emphasised the primary and over-riding importance of language maintenance. He wrote:

> But in order to keep the Irish language alive where it is still spoken, which is the utmost we can at present aspire to, nothing less than a house-to-house visitation and exhortation of the people themselves will do.

Eoin Mac Neill, who with Hyde was a founding member of the Gaelic League, and who was to a large extent the inspirational force behind the movement, believed that the revival could not be achieved through the agency of the school alone. In an article in *An Claidheamh Soluis*, 2 November 1900, he wrote:

> There can be no greater delusion than to imagine that a language can be kept alive alone by teaching. A language can have no real life unless it lives in the lives of the people.

His theory tended to underline the central importance of intergenerational transmission, which is now recognised as being the crucial element in achieving language revitalization. In his blueprint for the restoration of Irish, *Toghairm agus Gleus chum Oibre* in 1893, Mac Néill spelled out the significance of achieving linguistic transformation in the home, seeing it as being the key to revival. He wrote:

> A language has never survived, when it has not survived beside the fireplace. Even though teaching Irish is important, it is not the most important thing. The first thing we need to do then it to keep the language alive at the fireplace. (*The author's translation*)

O Growney who is also regarded as another ideological leader of the revival movement saw teaching the language, however, as the crucial element in its restoration. Like Hyde, O Growney did not envisage Irish ever supplanting English as the main language of the country. When referring to bilingualism in Wales, he wrote in *The Irish Ecclesiastical Record* (1890: 230):

> ... the children are taught the two languages concurrently the schoolbooks have Welsh and English on opposite pages and the children know English better than those in neighbouring English schools. That too is what those interested in Irish should aim at. It is not to banish English — that would be first of all, impossible, and absurd. Listen again to the words of Canon Farrar — 'Neither I nor any man in his senses dream for a moment of doing anything to hinder the universal prevalence of English. But the prevalence of English is very different from the exclusive dominance of it. We wish that every child should speak English perfectly and should also speak ... its native language perfectly.

When I spoke to people who went through the primary school system in the thirties and the forties, they would have attributed the way that Irish was 'pushed on them' to the legacy of Pearse's ideology in particular. A careful reading of Pearse's theories themselves, however, make for quite a different interpretation. Pearse espoused the value of learning Irish only within the context of a bilingualism. Having studied the cognitive effects of the bilingual method of teaching in Belgium and in Wales, he advocated that a similar approach be adopted in the *Gaeltacht* primary schools where all pupils should be taught Irish and English. Such an approach he also saw as being operable outside the *Gaeltacht* also. He firmly believed in the efficacy of the school system in achieving a language shift within the context of a bilingualism. He wrote:

> It has been doubted whether a language can really be learned at school. I

have satisfied myself by observation both in Ireland and in Belgium that it can. (Claidheamh Soluis, 23 January 1904)

If we look at the theories and ideologies of the early revivalists, we see quite conflicting ideas of the revival. While the Gaelic League in its earliest activities seemed to target the non-*Gaeltacht* population, it is interesting to note that the early theorists had associated the revival with language maintenance and with achieving a societal bilingualism. These theories were gradually lost sight of in the context of native governmental support and strategies, as I shall show in the next part of this paper.

Cultural Nationalism and Group (g) Function

It must be mentioned, however, that although there was a certain divergence in their opinions as to what constituted a language restoration, there was also some issues on which they were in agreement. From the early revivalists, *réamhchonraitheoirí* (prerevivalists), they would have inherited the academic cult of literary works in Irish.[1] Secondly, they all stressed the value of Irish as a means of remaining in communion with the past and as a way of counteracting the stresses engendered by modernisation.

In fact the background just outlined affords a certain comparison with the Hebrew situation. Cooper (1989) adopting Stewart's (1968) list of language functions, finds a similarity between the Irish and Hebrew situation in the group (g) function. This refers to the function of a linguistic system among the members of a single cultural or ethnic group. Linguistic and group membership is intrinsically linked, and language is perceived, therefore, as the key component in the criteria for group-membership definition.

This link between language and group membership was one of the central concerns of the élite who were to the forefront in the revival movement. Revivalists like Hyde, Mac Neill were in fact exponents of cultural nationalism, which stressed the intrinsic links between language and nationalism. Weinstein (1983) notes that these enthusiasts, espousing the Herderian belief in the existence of a separate language as a proof of nationhood, chose Irish as a symbol and as an instrument of efforts at political integration. Hence the protection of the language was verbalised and couched in defensive terms, advocating the rejection of assimilation. Similarly, in the case of Hebrew, a European-derived and Herderian-influenced language and nationality philosophy also evolved, highlighting Hebrew monolingualism as a key to participation in group membership of the Jewish nation which Zionism was proposing (Ben Yehuda, 1879).

However, the socio-political; factors using the same function (g) in both cases did not have similar effects due to historical circumstances. In the Irish case, Fishman (1972) points out that loyalty to the socio-political ideologies was confined to the participation of *protoelites* of upper middle-class individuals and organisations. Cultural nationalism at the end of the nineteenth century however, was a different type of nationalism from that which the Irish had espoused and had participated in, *en masse* earlier in the century. Comerford (1982) acknowledged that this type of nationalism had a strong palpable socio-economic dimension, particularly with its prospects of agrarian reform. The cultural nationalism to which De hIde and revivalists subscribed on the other hand, was neither governed nor motivated by socio-economics, and had little to offer the mass of the Irish population by way of financial gain, both inside and outside the *Gaeltacht*. It is not surprising, therefore, that the language and culture-agenda proposed by middle class enthusiasts had little to engage the imagination and needs of the masses.

One example of this class difference in response to cultural nationalism was the nature of participation in the Gaelic League itself. The Gaelic League was undoubtedly a successful cultural movement, in that within a short period, it had won wide support, in particular for its educational programme. However, MacNamara (1971) shows that the Gaelic League, nonetheless, failed to muster significant support among the working classes, with the main support for its 593 branches coming almost exclusively from middle-income groups. With the founding of the Free State in 1922, the thrust and nature of the ideology of language revival remained closely influenced by the cultural nationalism model, and proposals to revive the language on the basis of that model were largely alien to the culture and aspirations of the vast majority of the population. The national political factors were less successful in the case of Irish from then onwards, because economics competed with culture for the main ideology of the new state. Ó Doibhlin (no date) has commented, in fact, that it was the native government which dealt the greatest blow to the revival movement, by leaving it without its *raison d'être*. Successive government have formulated strategies down through the years aimed at promoting the extension of Irish outside the *Gaeltacht*, and the survival of the Irish-speaking areas in the remote areas along the western seaboard as distinctive speech communities has become a primary focus of policy intervention to maintain the language. It is now intended to look very briefly at some of these strategies of language planning in the early years.

Language Planning 1922–1930

One must now ask why revitalization did not occur in the case of Irish as happened in the case of Hebrew. To provide a satisfactory answer, one must examine the earliest efforts of the new state in status planning. The first aspect which springs to mind is that the government, while espousing wholeheartedly the Gaelic League's agenda, which had become more political in the years prior to self-independence, lost sight, however, of some of the theories of the early enthusiasts. The notion of a revival was gradually associated with promoting Irish monolingualism rather than achieving a societal bilingualism. This was probably due in no small part to the evolution of the Irish-Ireland movement that endeavoured to foster a culture and image that was diametrically opposed to all British influence. The centrality of intergenerational transmission was no longer stressed and education became the key to revival, as the government embarked on a dual policy of language maintenance and revival.

It is necessary at this point to briefly outline the developments in language planning in two areas in particular, namely, in the home domain and in education, and to illustrate that there was no intrinsic co-relation between both.

Intergenerational Transmission

There are regrettably few accounts of all Irish-speaking families outside the *Gaeltacht* in the early period. In fact, little attention, if any has been paid has been given to research in this area. It is my hope that my study of surviving members of all-Irish families from this early period over the coming months will begin to fill the void and provide some account of the socio-economic and affective factors involved in the deliberate linguistic change witnessed in these families.

One must say, of course, that the average family was not interested in discarding English in favour of Irish. Tierney writing as early as 1927 detected a cynicism and apathy among the general population to the notion of a revival. What had happened in practice, is that Irish, by the end of the 1920's, had become relegated to the mere symbolic role with its socio-political status weakened with the arrival of the free state. Even in ideological terms, the language by now was competing with English, which, of course had more attractive socio-economic appeal. Yet it was expected that people would change their language to Irish. Perhaps, the government might have misinterpreted cultural nationalism as being as cogent and as mobilising a force as economical nationalism, which of course was not the case. There are examples, however, from this early era that reflect the force of ideological revitalization.

Some families in Dublin and elsewhere motivated by strong socio-political ideology chose to become all-Irish speaking networks. As has been stated, earlier accounts of these families are few and fragmented. Bairéad (1967), gives us some insight into the language planning activities of one such Irish-speaking family in Dublin. Some planning was done to ensure that the children would continually and exclusively be exposed to Irish. Young girls from the *Gaeltacht* were employed as au pairs, to maximise exposure to the language in the daily transaction of daily life. Children attended Irish masses and church services. They were given Irish books to read and were sent to all-Irish schools. Here, in the schools, as one member of another all-such Irish family told me, they became aware for the first time of the dialectical and phonological variations in the language and were confused accordingly.

These networks were scattered and received little support because the state did not see the transmission of the language as the key and crucial factor affecting a revitalization (Fishman, 1991). They were often compared unfavourably to their English-speaking counterparts and neighbours. One such all-Irish speaker from this early period in Dublin spoke of how estranged and alien she felt among her English-speaking peers.

The New *Gaeltacht* Colonies

Efforts were also made at moving 122 Irish-speaking families from the western and the other *Gaeltachtaí* to form three new villages and agricultural settlements in the Co. Meath which is a eastern county adjacent to Dublin. This project was first mentioned by the *Gaeltacht* Commission in its report in 1926, which was established shortly after the state was founded, in order to investigate ways in which the language could be further maintained in the *Gaeltacht*. Having stressed how important socio-economic development was to linguistic maintenance policy, they formulated a policy that was to effect a language shift. In transplanting these Irish-speaking families from economically deprived background to richer pastures in Co. Meath, they hoped that this would result in a gradual spread of the language out into the hinterland of these villages. Thus, for the first time, maintenance and revivalist policies coalesced. Hindley (1990) has referred to this as a notable attempt at revival by transplantation. One contemporary source gives a clear statement of the objective entailed:

> They should form little villages. The language in these villages should be Irish, as the young men would naturally marry girls from near their original homes. The effect of such Irish-speaking, would, in time be bound to spread the language to the surrounding districts.

However, this extension of Irish did not occur. The Irish-speakers who were transplanted to the smallest of the communities at Allenstown quickly became assimilated with the English-speaking population. The families who arrived from the various *Gaeltacht*aí who settled in Baile Ghib (373 people) had eventually to revert to English as a lingua franca because of the mutually incomprehensible dialects. The more linguistically homogeneous community of Ráth Cairn, who came originally from the Connamara *Gaeltacht* has survived to this day but has had little if no effect in reversing the language shift to Irish in the hinterland community.

The Schools as Agents of Revival

There are two points to be made at the outset when referring to the schools as agents of revival. Firstly, the school-home link was not fostered and schools taught Irish without reference to language use particularly in home-neighbourhood domain. Secondly, the policies which were pursued, i.e., the promotion of monolingualism did not correspond with the original ideological theories of revival proposed and espoused by the Gaelic League enthusiasts.

Given the priority which the Gaelic League had given educational reform (Ó Súilleabháin, 1988) (Hyde, for example, had won the battle with the educational commissioners to ensure that Irish would become part of the curriculum and recognised for matriculation purposes); it is hardly surprising that the new State placed a special emphasis on the Irish language in its educational policies. In fact, the entire burden of the revival devolved on the schools. It was firmly believed that the language could be revived and revitalized by an effective system of teaching the language. Inherent in the policy of promoting the language in the school was an implicit understanding that as the schools were perceived as the main agents in effecting a language shift to English, the process could be reversed in favour of Irish.

In 1922, all national schools were instructed to teach Irish or to use it as a medium of instruction for at least half an hour a day. Subsequent policies were aimed at extending the use of Irish as a medium of instruction. The aim was to establish a *Gaeltacht* in each school. There was of course an implicit assumption about language knowledge leading to language use, i.e. that if children knew the language, they would speak it (Mac Mathúna, 1990). A similar immersion approach to what had been adopted in the schools in Palestine was also adopted here, although never fully realised. Ó Riagáin (1988) notes that the highest percentage of schools adopting a full immersion approach never reached more than 12 per cent of the entire school cohort (1940–1941).

It has been documented that the first teachers of Hebrew had a very limited knowledge of the language, even if they possessed a solid if passive knowledge in the biblical or talmudic varieties. Similarly, it was estimated that only 10 per cent of primary teachers had in fact some qualifications in Irish. As a result, intensive summer courses were set up, and in 1926, all-Irish preparatory colleges were established specifically for primary teachers.

Policy Implementation

In the early days, things looked hopeful and optimistic. Eoghan Mac Neill, who had once advocated that the language could not be revived through the agency of the school alone, and now minister for education, reported that the teaching of Irish was flourishing and reported positive effects from the teaching of the language (*Dáil Debates* XXI, 1923). It was not long, however, until teachers started to complain as they endeavoured to find out why exactly they were teaching the language. Were they teaching within the context of achieving a shift to monolingualism or achieving a societal bilingualism (*Dáil Debates* II 552)? They also complained that the content of the programme was too excessive and demanding and stressed that it had put pressure on teachers, especially on those who were not proficient enough to teach the language well.

At a conference of the Irish National Teachers Organisation in 1926, the Department yielding to the pressure, conceded that the time being devoted to the language was excessive and that full immersion should be mandatory, only where the children were able to follow the lessons profitably and easily.

Problems persisted, so much so, that by 1928, it was stated in the annual report of the Dept. of Education that:

> It appears that the aim of the present programme to impart to children a vernacular power over the language is not being approximately attained in the vast majority of schools outside the *Gaeltacht*.

There were constant allusions to the poor standard of Irish among teachers themselves and unfavourable comparisons were drawn between themselves and their counterparts in the *Gaeltacht*. In fact, unfavourable comparisons were constantly been drawn between speakers who had acquired Irish as L2 outside the *Gaeltacht* and the fluent and grammatically correct native speakers. Speakers who could not acquire the phonological system accurately were wont to be described disparagingly as not having the *blas* (the accent).

By 1928–1929, the Department of Education was despondent. In its report that year it stated:

> Outside the *Gaeltacht* the progress in the use of Irish as a medium of instruction is slow … children are not speaking Irish and I regret to say that I see no signs that we will witness a reverse of the situation unless we approach the issue with a different frame of mind. Good work was done in the early years but there is a decline in recent years.

So why did things develop in this way? One reason may well have been the confusion about the teaching of Irish in the absence of any clearly defined policy statement. At no stage was a pre-school component added, as happened in the case of Hebrew. Children on leaving school in the evening left Irish behind them, and, later, when they left school entirely, they grew out of the language. Secondly, an influential educationalist of the time was trying to abolish English by means of the educational system, namely, Rev. Corcoran who was professor of Education in University College, Dublin. He was highly influential and devoted his energies to espousing both the revival of Irish and the importance of Catholicism as a protection against what he perceived to be the atheistic influences of modernisation and liberalism. O Buachalla (1993) has commented that the system of primary education in particular bore the imprint of Corcoran's theories more than those of Pearse.

It is interesting to note what Corcoran wrote in 1925:

> Can the language be thus given in and through the school as a real vernacular? There is an abundance of historical evidence for an affirmative answer. It was in this way almost entirely that an English vernacular was enabled to replace the Irish tongue in Irish speaking Ireland. Over large portions of the country, this process of displacement developed from 1700 onwards through local schools. It was effective above all from 1830–1850 and these were the years that really counted. The reversal of the process is equally feasible, and without any draft on the vernacular practice of the home … The popular schools can give and can restore our native language. They can do it without positive aid from the home. (Corcoran, 1925: 386–387)

His overt denial of the importance of the home in achieving a language shift should be noted. Again, in another article, entitled, 'How the Irish Language Can be Revived', which appeared in the *Irish Monthly* in 1923 Corcoran had developed a rationale for the revival. He advocated that no English be taught — and that the *Modh Díreach* (the direct method), be employed in teaching the language. The inadequacies of this methodological approach, long associated with the teaching of Irish have been listed by Donmall (1991) and I think perhaps would be borne out by many a students' experience of learning the language within the school context.

It is my contention that while schools conferred a high status on the language, as schools did in the case of Hebrew, Irish children reacted negatively to it. Spolsky (1991) in proposing a model of language revitalization posits the relevance of L2 acquisition theory, in developing a workable model for understanding revitalization. He has stressed the importance of previous knowledge, ability motivation and learning as essential ingredients in language revival. All these aspects were by and large absent in the case of Irish in the home domain outside the *Gaeltacht*. While the intensive teaching continued, with full competence in the language at the end of primary school being the declared aim (*Dáil Debates* VII, 414, 3 July 1924), the language was not used in the home or community. This is hardly surprising because, unlike the Hebrew case, families in general had become alienated from the cultural nationalism model on which the revivalist premises were based. It was the teachers who were imposing the language on children against their will in an ideological vacuum.

Conclusion

In this paper I gave a brief historical perspective on the revival of Irish outside the *Gaeltacht* in the early period, in the hope of casting some light on some reasons why a language revitalization never occurred. It would appear that the theories and ideologies which governed language planning at this time were not focused enough on the exact form which a language revival would take. Government policies assumed erroneously that the Irish public outside the *Gaeltacht* espoused the cultural nationalism model which was the ideological base for such a revival. Clearly this was not the case, and language planning efforts, which were similar to Hebrew, in that they concentrated on gaining control of the school system were doomed to failure.

This perspective casts light however on the phenomenon of ideological revitalization, in that it refers to certain families in the Dublin area, for example, who managed to change the language of the home from English to Irish. Cooper (1989) sees a parallel with Hebrew here, referring to Ben Yehuda's efforts to inspire families in Jerusalem to use only Hebrew as the language of the home domain. Similar to the circle of Dublin all-Irish speaking families, the network in Jerusalem never extended to more than a mere handful of converts. These converts, in the case of Ireland, invariably came from the upper middle class stratum — the families of government ministers, civil servants and teachers.

The school-home link was never promoted assuming that language knowledge would simply lead to language use. In fact, there was never, to use a term used by Nahir (1988) a *great leap* in the revival of Irish, i.e. a spontaneous process of language revival which brought the language taught in the classrooms outside the school's walls on the lips of young people on the streets and roads and into the mouths of parents in the homes. This historical understanding of what went wrong, while emphasising the revival which still occurred, may have some significance for present language planning in Ireland.

At present the 1991 census returned a significant number, 32.5% of the population who self-reported to have some knowledge of Irish. However, the number who actually use Irish as the daily language of transaction is reported to be much lower. The 1991 census also returned 82,268 as being the population of the *Gaeltacht* and would have been included in the overall percentage. There are 113 all-Irish schools at present outside the *Gaeltacht* and 134 in the *Gaeltacht* itself. Again there are 171 *naíonraí* or all-Irish play schools outside the *Gaeltacht*. There also an upsurge in the numbers studying Irish at third level in recent times and Irish in the school curriculum no longer has a very narrow linguistic focus, referring now to language use, cultural awareness and to language awareness.[2]

However, the link between home and school as a step to achieving informal intergenerational oralcy within the current context of bilingualism needs to be studied. This may involve the verbalisation of socio-ideological factors which, may involve a status planning which takes cognisance of the positive aspect of increasing participation in Irish immersion programmes as an opportunity to raise an awareness of the prestigious role that language could play in youth culture.

There is a need for further research into the internal linguistic situation in the homes of children who attend all-Irish schools. The question still needs to be examined as to why and how a family in Ireland today would make a conscious effort to change the language in the home to Irish. The Hebrew case challenges us to re-examine the ideology within which Irish is taught in our schools. The Irish language revival movement has achieved much against all odds, but as we are now on the threshold of another revival, we need to study the domain of youth culture, so that the language, currently undergoing a positive revival among young people might, within the context of bilingualism begin to play a larger part in our identity and culture.

Notes

1. In fact Hutchinson (1987) classifies the revival movement at the end of the 19th century as being the third such revival or cultural renaissance movement.
2. Ó Laoire (1994: 33–9). See also Ó Laoire (1995, 1996).

References

Ben Yehuda, E (1879) Sheelah Nickbadah. Translated in E. Silberschlag (ed.) *(1981) Eliezer Ben Yehuda* (pp. 1–11). Oxford: Centre for Postgraduate Hebrew Studies.

Bairéad, S. (1967) *Feasta* (pp. 5–8). Meán Fómhair.

Comerford, R.V. (1982) Míshuaimhneas agus náisiúnachas sa naoú haois déag. *Léachtaí Cholm Chille* XIII, 151–65. Maigh Nuad, An Sagart.

Cooper, R. L. (1989) *Language Planning and Social Change*. New York: Cambridge University Press.

Corcoran, T, (1925) The Irish language in Irish schools. *Studies*.

Daly, D. (1974) *The Young Douglas Hyde*. Dublin: National University Press.

Dorian, N. (1987) *Language Death: The Life Cycle of a Scottish Gaelic Dialect*. Philadelphia: University of Pennsylvania Press.

Donmall, G. (1991) Old problems and new solutions: Language awareness work in GCSE foreign language classrooms. In C. James and P. Garrett (eds) *Language Awareness in the Classroom*. London: Longman.

Fishman, J.A. (1972) *Language and Nationalism: Two Integrative Essays*. Newbury, MA.

— (1991) *Reversing Language Shift*. Berlin: Mouton.

Hindley, R. (1990) *The Death of the Irish Language*. London: Routledge.

Hutchinson, J. (1987) *The Dynamics of Cultural Nationalism*. London: Allen and Unwin.

Hyde, D. (1886) A plea for the Irish language. *Dublin University Review*, August, pp. 35–7.

— (1894) The necessity for de-anglicising Ireland. In Sigerson, Duffy and Hyde (eds) *The Revival of Irish Literature* (pp. 117–61). London: Allen and Unwin.

— (1906) The great work of the Gaelic League. *San Francisco Leader*, 17 February.

Mac Mathúna, L. (1990) Thirty years a-floundering? Official policy and community use of Irish in the Republic of Ireland 1956–1986. In B. Bramsbäck (ed.) *Homage to Ireland: Aspects of Culture, Literature and Language*. Uppsala: Almqvist and Wiksell.

MacNamara, J. (1971) Successes and failures in the movement for the restoration of Irish. In J. Rubin and B.H. Jernudd (eds) *Can Language Be Planned? Sociolinguistic Theory and Practice for Developing Nations*. Honolulu: University of Hawaii.

Mac Néill, E. (1900) Toghairm agus gleus chum gluasachta na Gaedhilge do chur ar aghaidh i nÉirinn. *Irisleabhar na Gaeilge*, 4 March, 177–9.

Nahir, M. (1988) Language planning and language acquisition: The great leap in the Hebrew revival. In C.B. Paulston (ed.) *International Handbook of Bilingualism and Bilingual Education* (pp. 275–95). New York: Greenwood Press.

Ó Buachalla, S. (1993) Idéalachas teanga agus oideachas an Phiarsaigh Prút, L. *Dúchas*. Coiscéim 7–25.

Ó Cuiv, B. (1969) The Gaelic cultural movements and the new nationalism. In K.B. Nowlan (ed.) *The Making of 1916*. Dublin: Oifig an tSoláthair.

Ó Doibhlin, B (no date) Súil siar ar an athbheochan. *I Aistí Critice agus Cultúir*. Dublin, FNT, 217–35.

Ó Growney, E. (1890) The national language. *Irish Ecclesiastical Record*, November.

Ó Laoire, M. (1994) Spleácadh ar mhúineadh na Gaeilge san iarbhunscoil. *Teangeolas* 33, 33–9.

— (1995) Athbheocham Teanga Scéal na hEabhraise agus na Gaeilge 1880–1930. Unpublished Ph.D. thesis. National University of Ireland, Maynooth.

— (1996) Hebrew and Irish: Language revival revisited. In T. Hickey and J. Williams (eds) *Language Education and Society in a Changing World*. Clevedon: Multilingual Matters.

Ó Riagáin, P. (1988) Bilingualism in Ireland 1973–1983: An overview of national sociolinguistic surveys. *International Journal of the Sociology of Language* 70, 29–52.

Ó Súilleabháin, D. (1988) *Cath na Gaeilge sa Chóras Oideachais 1893–1911*. Dublin: Conradh na Gaeilge.

Stewart, W. (1968) A sociolinguistic typology for describing national multilingualism. In J. Fishman (ed.) *Readings in the Sociology of Language*. The Hague: Mouton.

Spolsky, B. (1991) Hebrew language vitalization within a general theory of second language learning. In R. Cooper and B. Spolsky (eds) *The Influence of Language on Culture and Thought* (pp. 137–57). Berlin: Mouton de Gruyter. .

Tierney, M. (1927) The revival of the Irish language. *Studies* Vol. XVI, 1–22.

Weinstein B. (1983) *The Civic Tongue: Political Consequences of Language Choices*. New York: Longman.

The Debate

Nigel Reeves (Aston University): You have stressed the use of Irish at 'the fireplace' as being very important for language survival but if Irish today is to be useful for anything other than domestic, every day purposes it needs to be part of the information age and to encompass medicine, technology, science, and other aspects of contemporary culture. It cannot aspire to be a medium of instruction in the schools unless the question of terminology has been faced. How does one produce an Irish terminology for all these scientific, technological subjects?

Muiris Ó Laoire (University College Galway): The terminology institute in Dublin works continuously on new words and structures. How seriously it is taken is a different question. Traditionally, these prescriptive initiatives don't seem to have a great deal of success.

Lewis Glinert (SOAS London): I've noted this very phenomenon in the Israeli context. There was great resistance to the Language Committee at the beginning of the century, and the Academy which took over from it in 1953 has not fared much better.

Sue Wright (Aston University): I think the success of language academies is linked to purism — a requirement of speakers to speak the language without fault. When there is any outside threat to the language there seems to be a knee jerk reaction: on the one hand to safeguard 'standards' (in all the word's meanings), and on the other to put up fences against borrowings. This is exactly what has happened, and is happening with French, faced with the onslaught of English. The French feel the need to ban borrowed terms; it was actually made illegal by the Toubon law to use borrowed words in public language. At the same time there is a national commitment to the norm; dictation is a national sport with the finals of competitions shown on prime time TV.

Lewis Glinert: I have to take issue with this. I think there are ample cases of languages which are willing to incorporate vast amounts of foreign lexical material into the language, yet wish for, and need, respect for the norm. A classic case of this now is Yiddish in the English speaking world; a Yiddish speaking society uses all English technological terms and has no problem with this but still wishes respect for the norm.

Ken George (University of Plymouth): Japanese is a good example of using foreign terminology, and I understand that it has very few words of Japanese origin for technological terms. And, whereas now it is English, it used to be Chinese. At the same time there is great respect for the norm.

Nigel Reeves: But these are secure speech communities that have no problem with absorbing and assimilating alien terms. We are talking, in the Irish case, about a precarious speech community that could be alienated and flooded by foreign terms.

Frank Knowles (Aston University): What is the motivation for corpus planning

— is it a desire for transparency of meaning or is it, in the desire to have one's *own* term, an expression of linguistic insecurity?

Bernard Spolsky (Bar-Ilan University): It is not a problem for the speakers; it is a problem for the self-conscious purists. It becomes critical if the revival takes place in a self-conscious educational environment. In the Hebrew context people complain in theory about the use of borrowed terminology. In practice speakers have no problem with these terms but do have problems with the transparent terms that the Academy invents. I agree with Lewis Glinert's earlier comment. If you do not add this conscious concern over borrowed terms, things will work.

Muiris Ó Laoire: In Ireland neither the Gaeltacht community nor Irish speakers outside the Gaeltacht have a problem with loan terms.

Julian Edge (Aston University): The absence of links between the learning approach and institutions is very important here. The argument seems to be that the fireside approach is better than the school environment; it would follow that the speech community is more important and influential here than the Academy. But it may well be that both influences exist, are interacting with each other, and add to the vitality of the whole language situation, and one without the other is much poorer.

Bernard Spolsky: I was wondering what sort of language was being used, and what functions were involved in the teaching material used in the 1920s in Ireland?

Muiris Ó Laoire: The language used was semi-literary, the language of the home came later in the 1950s.

Frank Knowles: In the teaching materials used in the 1920s and 30s, was it the Celtic alphabet that was used, and was this a factor in the struggle of the revival?

Muiris Ó Laoire: This is an interesting question because people decry to this day the use of the Latin alphabet. It did not seem as if children in the classroom experienced any particular difficulty with the Celtic script, and it was seen to be an integral part of the Irish language. The script became more simplified in the 1950s, and there was the development of corpus planning. In the classroom the method known as AVC was divided into three parts: the first involved structures which were drilled, the second part consisted of set conversation pieces which were learned by rote, and the third part was creativity which a lot of teachers never actually arrived at, where the structure would have been used in new situations. The work mainly concentrated on oral skills, and was taught by the Direct Method. In this educational setting, reading and writing the Celtic script may have added some difficulties.

Charlotte Hoffmann (Salford University): Is there a generally accepted standard dialect?

Muiris Ó Laoire: No, there is not and this does present a problem, particularly for learners of Irish who are presented with three distinct dialectical systems. There is, however, a standard written Irish.

Charlotte Hoffmann: Was the dialect that was promoted at the beginning different to the ones found in the Gaeltacht?

Muiris Ó Laoire: Yes, it was quite different. For example, it has a different phonological system from many of the dialects. Many of the teachers in the early days did not have knowledge or confidence in the normativised language, which also had profound effects on language in the classroom.

In the past, dialect divergence was confined to the Gaeltacht, but now modern Irish is beginning to develop more independently, and there is emerging in Dublin a distinct dialect, used above all by young Dubliners speaking Irish. This has, of course, been disparaged by the purists, but I feel it is a true sign of some vitality.

Lewis Glinert: What were the attitudes and motivations which formed the base line *vis-à-vis* Irish culture and language at the beginning of the revival movement?

Muiris Ó Laoire: The early activists espoused the revival of the language through a link with the past, preserving the culture and the ideology, and rejecting assimilation. The masses did not participate in the ideology as such but they did have a clear understanding of the movements and political change at the turn of the century. Using Irish may have been something which at the beginning they were very proud to do, but which quickly disappeared, as it lost its political significance when Ireland became a Free State. I do not feel they were fully conscious of the cultural significance of the language. Cultural motivation seems to be sidelined, and can only be afforded or visualised by very few.

Curriculum development in schools has now taken cognisance of this, and is promoting culture awareness. There is a drive for children in English medium primary schools to become aware of the Irish language and Irish literature through translation. The Irish syllabus in secondary education always had a strong literary bias because it was hoped that a love of literature would underpin the spoken language. There is still a strong emphasis on the study of literature in both linguistic traditions. Now teachers tend to concentrate on short stories, novels or poetry by contemporary writers. There is a youth culture developing in Irish, partially promoted through this lively literary tradition, and partially a spontaneous movement.

Helen Kelly-Holmes (Aston University): I would like you to expand on the development of the Irish language media: the new television channel, the radio, the newspapers.

Muiris Ó Laoire: The Irish language TV channel which is planned to start in 1996/7 has encountered some resentment due to its cost and its effect on taxes. Once this reluctance has been conquered, the next hurdle will be to attract an audience which spans all age groups; we must be very careful to attract young people, to express youth culture. If this channel is only seen as something for older people, then it will play no role in maintaining the language.

Helen Kelly-Holmes: Taking the public with you on the language question is quite hard in the Republic. What is your opinion on recent curriculum development in Irish, and the whole notion of the Gaelscoileanna? Why has it been seen so negatively?

Muiris Ó Laoire: I think the Gaelscoileanna movement came as a surprise. It started in the early 1980s, and had very committed followers, and used the immersion approach. Initially success was slow, but gradually parents began to see the advantages of these schools, which were not necessarily linguistic. There were smaller classes, more equipment. MacNamara had argued that the immersion approach would retard progress in other key subjects such as maths. However, new research findings from Canada, in the late 1970s and 1980s, seriously undermined such beliefs, and showed that there were very many other variables at work in some immersion situations, which, in fact, made immersion submersion, and it was these non-linguistic factors which caused the negative results in other subjects. Research is now being carried out to see what are the outcomes in Ireland — scholastically within the education system, and linguistically within society. What is happening linguistically outside the school? It might be that we are on the threshold of something new.

John Rex (University of Warwick): How does language relate to the problems in Northern Ireland? I'd be interested to know if the language question is of concern to the Republicans and Nationalists. Is there strong support for Irish in Northern Ireland?

Muiris Ó Laoire: Nationalists do pay attention to the language question. In fact the language has been acquired by many in the Nationalist community, and the motivation for this is obviously political. A particularly telling example of this is the prisoners who were interned and used their prison term to acquire Irish. There is a need to do more research on this, however. A situation of armed conflict over decades hasn't made it easy to set up studies — and of course reliable and objective data on language use would be hard to acquire in the Northern Irish situation.

There are language policies in Northern Ireland to make space for Irish: these allow for bilingual signs; for Irish medium education (in Belfast there is an all-Irish school); for Irish as a subject in the National Curriculum.

And, historically, the shift to English of the Northern Irish was slower than that of their counterparts in the South, possibly due to Catholic members of the community holding positions that did not require the use of English. Also it would be wrong to think that the Irish language was exclusively the province of the Catholics; the Scottish landowners brought with them a Scottish Gaelic, very close on the dialect continuum to some Northern Irish dialects.

John Rex: Has there been a version of Irish linguistic nationalism which was perhaps trying to perpetuate a reactionary type of society?

Muiris Ó Laoire: Yes, what occurred was the image of the speaker in the Gaeltacht as a rural, Catholic, traditionalist peasant. In parts of the Republican movement this model was advanced as the 'perfect' Irishman; this was the romantic philosophy of the *Irish Ireland* model. In reality, for the great mass of the population, this image was very complex. Many people responded with a curious mixture of admiration and superiority.

Helen Kelly-Holmes: The negative attitude towards these people is illustrated by the pejorative term 'gaelgeóirí', which was used to refer to those who wore a fáinne ring to indicate that they wished to be addressed in Irish. They had little tolerance of bilingualism or patience with the less than perfect speaker of Irish.

This negativity together with their conservative outlook was transferred to the image of the language in many people's minds.

Bernard Spolsky: This is the exact opposite of the Zionist youth secular modernist movement.

John Rex: Irish emigration in this century and the last, to other parts of the world, has resulted in what we could term the Irish diaspora. To what extent do those who have emigrated attempt to keep the language alive?

Muiris Ó Laoire: There is a lot more data on this question: emigrants and language maintenance have been widely studied in a number of settings, particularly the language shift amongst the Irish in America. I've done work myself in Massachusetts where there is still a strong Gaeltacht community. Although in general it is mainly the older people who have retained cultural and linguistic links, the younger generations are more culturally aware than their counterparts in Ireland, and perhaps more enthusiastic about the language.

Helen Kelly-Holmes: Do you think that the policy for defending the language whereby certain professions need to take an Irish language examination has helped maintenance or is it simply viewed as a token gesture?

Muiris Ó Laoire: The regulation was put in place because of a belief that it would lead to language use. However, I do not think it has helped greatly, because the students are merely sitting the examinations for the sake of the qualification, not to be able to speak the language. Perhaps in the case of certain civil servants, their knowledge of the language has developed because it is something they use, for example in legal drafting.

John Rex: I think it is necessary in this discussion of the revival of the Irish language to look at how it was killed off in the first place. Irish was obliterated ruthlessly and deliberately by the English who imposed the English language on the population. How did they do this?

Muiris Ó Laoire: There was a combination of factors which led to English being the dominant language. To begin with, Irish was maintained by the English. For example, there was a translation of the Bible, and Irish was used in the parliament. However, later on in the occupation it was decided to replace Irish with English, probably in an attempt to simplify matters of state, rather than for ideological reasons. The schools were important in the shift since English became the medium of instruction, and students learned not only the language but also the cultural baggage, the literature, poetry etc. Two other factors were important: the famine played a major role in the transition; on the one hand, there was literal language death in the sense that the speakers died, while on the other, the famine led to a huge wave of emigration particularly from the Irish speaking areas. The destinations were the English speaking countries, Australia, America, England.

Helen Kelly-Holmes: The long-term significance of this meant that from the middle of the nineteenth century, parents tended to prepare their children for emigration by making them learn English. Irish became associated with the poverty and misery of the famine.

Stephen Barbour (Middlesex University): In terms of speakers, Welsh is now in a better position than Irish. Religion may be a factor here. In Ireland, since the majority of the population was Catholic, and the mass was said in Latin, and reading of the Bible was not encouraged in Irish, religion did little to encourage Irish. This contrasts strongly with Wales where there was great encouragement for the Protestant population to read the Bible in Welsh and attend services in their own language. Do you think this had an effect?

Muiris Ó Laoire: Certainly. As you point out, religion did not play any part in the revival movement. Priests during their training spoke English and therefore would also preach in English. However, the contrasting roles of religion are perhaps more complex than your dichotomy allows. Religion was not so important at the beginning of the independence, but it became so later.

Helen Kelly-Holmes: Another point which should be taken into consideration is the role of the Anglo-Irish in the revival of the language and awareness of culture.

Sue Wright: Almost all nineteenth century linguistic nationalism was promoted by a bourgeois or upper class. In many cases members did not speak the language and needed to acquire it. Is there anything to say about the role of class in revival, revitalization, maintenance in Ireland today?

Helen Kelly-Holmes: Yes, there seems to be. The Gaelscoileanna and the older 'A' or Irish-medium schools have always been supported by the educated middle-class — many of them teachers. However, in Northern Ireland, the movement to learn Irish is very much a working class phenomenon.

Sue Wright: In all the contexts we have discussed, the fundamental question has to be: why maintain societal diglossia? What are the social and economic costs of bilingualism? And what do we actually lose when we move to monolingualism? What do we gain when we promote bilingualism in a society which is on its way to monolingualism?

Frank Knowles: Is there not a prior question which is, what does it cost not to maintain two languages in a society?

Bernard Spolsky: I have yet to find an economically-based model which takes into account the value of knowing a language other than the majority language.

Nigel Reeves: There may not be models for this but *de facto* the market place gives us indications of worth. For example, AT & T's language line interpreting service shows the economic value of the languages for which it provides. People are willing to pay for this language knowledge. This is very different from the humanitarian liberal views that we try to present.

Bencie Woll (City University): You could, however, argue that by maintaining a language for non-economic reasons, for example, to preserve cultural diversity, there may in fact be an indirect economic dimension. The most obvious example here is tourism. This may not be possible to measure, and one might argue that it is token folklorism rather than revival.

Nigel Reeves: One case study where interesting personal decisions have been made about language use is the Iranian community in California, a large affluent society, who have access to their own media and newspapers, where many do not speak English because there is no need, and where they can be said to have their own economy to a certain extent, in that they are self sufficient. Within that community are those that act as an 'interface', they speak English, are in power, entrepreneurial in spirit, and perhaps came from a more privileged background in the country of origin. I believe that the amount of bilingualism here is being kept to the minimum for economic reasons. The Iranian community accepts that it is a world with in a world, and considerable savings of effort — if not money — are made by not attempting bilingualism for all.

John Rex: Value here is being turned into a question of profitability. I think that I want to probe for an answer not in economic terms. If I ask Sue's question again I might get answers that would try to define the nature of ethnic groups at the simplest level. It seems that there are a number of things — kinship, neighbour-hood, sharing a common language, religion, having contact with the ancestors, myth of origin etc. — all of which equal ethnicity, and this has a peculiar appeal as being emotionally uplifting, sacred etc. I am interested in the question of what contribution sharing a language has to that, what it contributes to creating an ethnic group. One school of opinion, typified by Arthur Schlesinger, claims that the wonder of the United States is that all the immigrant groups have become one, and that essentially they have a European culture. According to his reading, the US is a new nation with English as its language, and this nation is threatened by two sources, a rhetorical black secessionism and the Hispanic demand for bilingualism. This, in his opinion, will destroy the US.

Frank Knowles: This applies equally to the current situation in the former Soviet Union, as stated in 'Soviet Disunion' which views the post-Soviet context in exactly the same way as Schlesinger.

Lewis Glinert: Going beyond language simply as a symbol of group identity, language can be an agent of group identity, a vehicle for a shared oral culture or a shared literary canon. Perhaps the time has gone when we can really expect the educational system to give the children who might be taught an ethnic language that kind of cultural competence. I don't know if at the end of the twentieth century children will have any wish or time to learn classical texts. What will be the consequences of this for the language and the literary tradition if this is the case?

Sue Wright: Putting texts into print demands so much capital, that the literary tradition of the written text has often worked against minority languages. Print capitalism demanded large markets. Perhaps as we enter the phase of multi-media this will mean it will become possible to produce and distribute texts more cheaply and cater for smaller numbers of speakers and readers. It depends on how available and accessible this technology is.

Mike Grover (Multilingual Matters): The class difference in language mainte-nance is going to be replicated in a slightly different way in the future as it is only affluent societies that are going to be able to permit themselves a kind of multilingualism through this technology. Then there will be other societies who will not be able to buy into this type of technology.

Nigel Reeves: But of course a different type of culture, a new culture will be transmitted by new media. A lot of radio stations are broadcasting in the lesser-used languages. Many are youth programmes, interactive, community orientated, and I believe this niche in the market is booming. The technology is making it cheap and viable for small interest groups to get together whether it be for linguistic or other interests.

Bencie Woll: I have had some involvement with the BBC's educational division which deals with programmes for ethnic minorities and the deaf community. People in these communities feel that these programmes are not always youth orientated. They are for the most part traditional and unattractive to young people.

Bernard Spolsky: It is all a question of control. Take for example the Maoris who claimed access to media under the terms of the Treaty of Waitangi. A Maori radio station set up under this policy that played rock music rather than traditional Maori music attracted a wide audience of young people and was very successful. There were many complaints: from the business community because it was taking away advertising from the other stations; from sections of the Maori community because it was not promoting the aspects of Maori culture which they had expected. This makes clear that even when it is possible for ethnic groups to gain access to media what that access will bring will not necessarily be the traditional heritage. It will be the new global culture, which was not the intention of the activists when they demanded this access.

Muiris Ó Laoire: Should we be obliged to distil our culture and traditions through the language of youth culture?

Julian Edge: You made a point in your paper about the lack of interest in the language by the students you were teaching. Surely that could be the response to be expected from this age group?

Helen Kelly-Holmes: I think that the situation of the Irish language is particular. The attitude to learning languages such as French and German is very enthusiastic; it is specifically the Irish language which students are not keen to learn. Learning the languages of the European Union has been painted in very positive economic terms.

Charlotte Hoffmann: If you are committed to societal bilingualism, you have to make things available in both languages so that people have a choice, and don't feel engineered by others. It is expensive but only by doing this can you ensure that there is vitality. If there is a dip in interest among young people for a period, isn't there a case for continuing to provide both the languages because attitudes may change.

Bencie Woll: I think there is also this notion of role models. Young people need to be presented with figures who reflect their culture, and who they can identify with, rather than someone who is simply regarded as preaching at them. This is always a factor in the success of minority language programmes, and I think this also relates to a point that Professor Spolsky made, that it was not only the way Hebrew was taught that was important but who was actually teaching it. Youth need to identify with speakers.

Stephen Barbour: This brings us back to issues of power and authority. One generation may view the prescriptions of another generation as being foisted upon them. There is a class issue which comes across very clearly in the Irish situation; a relatively secure economic elite is in danger of prescribing to everyone else how they should see their ethnicity. And then there is the question of being able to afford to be bilingual. Large numbers, for instrumental reasons, want to focus on the language with economic power. This can be the result of a misperception, but foisting bilingualism upon them will not necessarily convince them otherwise. We know that bilingualism can be a resource, but there can be these different perspectives depending on the economic position of people.

Julian Edge: This is the perennial, classic problem: bilingualism perceived as a luxury that cannot be afforded. However, the people who are prepared to use their children as fodder for their own ideological commitment would be quite unusual, but also very strong and likely to be successful, and this will show through in family achievement.

Sue Wright: The statistics for bilinguals from ethnic minority communities in British universities in fact bear this out.

John Rex: So we have actual data that contradicts the argument that if immigrants want to get on they should forget their language and culture, and concentrate on being English speakers! But I don't think we should overemphasise this. There are other possibilities in this situation in modern society — the maintenance of the communal language creates a bond which may make mobility harder for the majority of the group. So you start getting solidarity as a method of defence. Then the minority language may become a vehicle for a kind of class solidarity, and this militates against success in the dominant culture and against socio-economic mobility.

Sue Wright: When we come to language and solidarity there is a danger of treating groups as monoliths, both in real terms and in research terms, and they are not. We have discussed this pitfall before in these seminars. From the available studies it is clear that some members of a group may benefit from their bilingualism in the British context; some will not.

Frank Knowles: What you have said there is that the economic aspects are the independent variant, and language is the dependent.

Stephen Barbour: I think that is usually so. It is difficult to ignore economic pressure. This means that an important place for language transmission is the work place. In areas of Catalunya there is now evidence that young people who don't have Catalan as a mother tongue are likely to acquire Catalan in their teenage years at work. Another example of the importance of acquisition at work is low German. We shouldn't be lured into thinking that the education system is the be all and end all.

Sue Wright: Well, if in a society there is the private language and the public, the education system is unlikely to play a totally unambiguous role in promoting the private language because unless you have at the end of an education system, access into the work place which uses the 'private' language, the education system must prepare its students for their working life, and, therefore, abandon the minority language. In fact the role of education is linked closely to employment, and you can't deal with it separately.

Ken George: I think the situation in Brittany is relevant here. It is very interesting to see how those committed to teaching Breton are also raising the profile of

English with the view to attracting more students to schools that promote both. The doubt that there is a social role for a bilingual French-Breton speaker is pitted against the idea that linguistic competence can be promoted across the board. In Brittany no one under the age of about fifty speaks Breton, and in another twenty years it will be in a parlous state. This situation was foreseen in the 1970s, and so a body, the Diwan, was set up to provide education from the age of three. All subjects would be taught through the medium of Breton. One of the goals of this system is to incorporate the Diwan type school into the French system, to make the government recognise that an education can, and should, be provided through this medium. By doing so they are diametrically opposing the policy of the government, which is to recognise no other language than French. The Breton schools cater for 1% of the school population. However, the Diwan schools have had some effect outside their actual confines; there are some Breton classes available in the non-Diwan schools.

Sue Wright: And teacher training colleges now provide the opportunity to prepare for Breton as a subject.

Ken George: If one can make an assumption that education includes nursery age children then the language medium is very significant. The distinction between in class and playground is blurred.

Lewis Glinert: Looking at things in terms of cohorts of children gradually passing through the machine, brings me back to a point in Muiris' paper which I feel relates also to the Hebrew experience. The term 'hearth language' tends to lead to the assumption that the hearth language is the language between child and parent but from informed speculation about what happened with the Hebrew movement, it may have been elder siblings to younger siblings, bearing in mind that we are speaking about children who were active and spent a lot of time outside playing.

Ken George: When children start to play in the threatened language a significant goal has been reached in the revitalization.

Stephen Barbour: I would like to introduce a word of caution, some of the strongest vernacular languages in Europe have not featured traditionally in the education system, for example Luxemburgish and Swiss German. In both these cases it is possible to argue, of course, that they are not independent languages. I understand in Luxembourg that in the past children were expected to function straight away in German. Luxemburgish still remained vibrant, however, and even kept its own written form. And I ought to add that the language situation in education has changed slightly recently.

John Rex: Should the state finance the education of minority languages? Is it best done in the school or through supplementary classes?

Charlotte Hoffman: It depends on the minorities you are speaking about. In Spain where there are clear minorities, and education fulfils a very important role in the regional areas, it would be political suicide for a government not to fund minority education and keep it in the mainstream. In the fascist era it was suppressed but under a democratic system it couldn't be.

Alexandra Korol (University of Manchester): The Dutch government decided in the early 1990s that language and cultural maintenance for minority groups constituted by recent immigration should be financed by the government, but outside the main school curriculum. This is a reasonable solution in that it gives children a chance to maintain their language and identity, and also to follow the same curriculum as their peers. There can be no excuse for the host country providing two tier education, and two tier destinations at the end. This need to be like the mainstream, to benefit from mainstream society which has the economic weight, and the desire to maintain cultural and linguistic specificity will always cause tension within linguistic minorities

Bencie Woll: Also relating to this issue we need to consider whether the people who are available to teach the minority language, have the same training and status as that of the teachers the government appoint to deliver other parts of the curriculum, and also whether there exist traditional methods of teaching which are very much at variance with the ethos of how curriculum is structured, and education is delivered, in the school system. If you get conflict here, then there is almost certainly a situation destined for failure. And, yet, if the teachers of the minority language have to be from the mainstream tradition then that may bar perfectly good teachers who have come through a different system, and be experienced as racism.

Manjula Datta (University of North London): Politically speaking I think that home language support should be provided in schools because once it is accepted that it is not the schools' responsibility then this gives all sorts of negative messages: it cannot be important because it is not on the school premises; it cannot be important because it is not in the curriculum; it cannot be important because it is not in the examination system. The speakers of languages which do not appear in the mainstream education system are going to conclude that these languages are not valued by the wider community. The signal is very clear about the comparative educational/economic worth of Urdu and French, for example. However, I would settle for resources for language being diverted to community language schools, if that were all that was on offer. It is important that such resources should include training of the teachers because children are disadvantaged if they face a conflict of styles.

Bernard Spolsky: There is no evidence of any success of language maintenance through the after school Hebrew programmes. In terms of developing competence of any level in the spoken language, the programmes produce minimal results in most parts of the world. To really produce a generation that maintains or revives a language takes an enormous amount of effort, much more than can be provided in those programmes, I think. It is a whole society process. However, as a first step, one of the critical things in language policy is for the school to accept the existence of the language. The minimal commitment that one could ask from the school is that it recognises that the other languages exist, and if it teaches another language, that it does it adequately rather than replacively.

When a school is taking a replacive attitude, and saying to the children 'go home and tell your parents they must stop speaking their language to you, otherwise you won't make it', it creates an impossible conflict. If the school is more tolerant, it is possible to set up a situation where the school tolerates and respects the interests of the other language. When the language maintenance has the support of the school, the community and the home there is a good chance of success. But where any of those elements are missing there is likely to be failure in language maintenance or language revitalization.

Muiris Ó Laoire: The reasons people from different area backgrounds have given for language behaviour open up a whole range of possibilities as to why people choose to change the language of the home. Ritual reinstatement of the language by society as a whole does not seem to be the answer to language revitalization or at least not the whole answer. But after all of this, I don't know that we are any closer to identifying a point in the language revitalization process where it is possible to predict what is going to happen thereafter.

Bernard Spolsky: To be able to make predictions, we need a model with only what is relevant to the issue. We must be careful to differentiate between language shift, language maintenance, language revival, language revitalization. What they all have in common is that a weaker language is trying to survive faced with a stronger language, but in other respects there are important differences. I don't think we have fallen into the trap of being too linguacentric, and not categorising the many different forces that are relevant, but I don't think we have tamed them into a model — or indeed models. We do know they are there, now we must work on the interactions.

The world as a whole does seem to be pulling in two directions. On the one hand, there is the pull towards unification, in that there is a certain globalisation of culture; on the other hand, the continued vigour of local, traditional cultures is clear. Language seems to be a good starting point from which to study this dual pull.

And finally, I am still left with the original puzzle over whether Hebrew is a special case.